# Singapore

## DIRECTIONS

WRITTEN AND RESEARCHED BY

**Mark Lewis**

NEW YORK • LONDON • DELHI

www.roughguides.com

# Contents

# Introduction to Singapore

**It was the immense changes that the twentieth century imposed upon the tiny city state of Singapore that transformed it from a sleepy colonial backwater into the bustling, futuristic shrine to consumerism that is so familiar today. This is a city in permanent flux: cranes peep from above the skyline like watchful meerkats and fresh skyscrapers and shopping complexes rise up at a scarcely believable rate. Yet visitors prepared to peer beneath its ultra-modern surface will still discover dusty temples, fragrant medicinal shops and colonial buildings, and enduring values and traditions. Nor is Singapore, in reality, a concrete jungle: the island boasts an abundance of parks, nature reserves, and lush, tropical greenery.**

Much of Singapore's fascination stems from its multicultural population. Immigration has shaped the destiny of this small island, the work ethic of its settlers turning it into an Asian economic powerhouse whose influence far outweighs its size. First to step ashore, in 1819, were the seafaring explorers of the British East India Company; soon after, the duty-free port they established began to attract migrants from across Asia, particularly from China, India and the Malay Peninsula. Almost two hundred years later, the resulting mix of cultures richly textures the island, turning a short walk into what seems like a hop from one continent to another.

## When to visit

No time of year is really better than any other to visit Singapore. Just 136km north of the equator, the island is hot and sticky throughout the year. Be prepared for rain – November and December are usually the wettest months, though they are also the coolest. On average, June, July and August record the lowest annual rainfall.

▲ Surfer at East Coast Park

Despite the rampant rate of change, it remains possible to experience customs, traditions and religious practices that remain unchanged from the early days of colonial rule. Lion dancing troupes gambol through the streets of Chinatown during Chinese New Year, as they always have. Indians still light oil lamps outside their homes to celebrate Deepavali, the festival of lights. And Malays continue to gather together during the Muslim fasting month of Ramadan to break their fast with traditional cakes and snacks after nightfall.

One of the greatest pleasures of visiting Singapore, and another happy by-product of the convergence of cultures, is the opportunity to sample the vast range of mouthwatering Asian cuisines the island has to offer. In Singapore, it's possible to breakfast on Indian roti bread and curry sauce, lunch on Chinese dim sum and dine on delicious Malay *nasi campur*.

Singaporean culture is by no means backward-looking, however. The growth of its arts scene in recent years has been remarkable, exemplified

▼ Peranakan houses on Koon Seng Road, Joo Chiat

▲ Shoppers on Orchard Road

by the opening of the wondrous Esplanade – Theatres on the Bay project, in 2002, which gave the island a new cultural focal point. Theatres, galleries, cinemas and other arts spaces flourish across the island, their output often informed by the communal Asian experience. Complementing all this is a burgeoning drinking and nightlife scene that recently received the ultimate seal of approval with the opening of a new post for the global clubbing brand, *Ministry of Sound*.

The appeal of Singapore stretches beyond the city limits, though. Surreally in this most modern of states, a pocket of primary rainforest survives in the centre of the island, allowing outward-bound visitors to trek under a primeval forest canopy and come face to face with tropical wildlife. Elsewhere, there are expanses of golden sands to enjoy; and, on the satellite island of Ubin, meandering tracks and sleepy kampung villages unaltered in fifty years.

▲ The CBD and Boat Quay

# Singapore
## AT A GLANCE

### The Colonial District

The spires, colonnades, domes, and lawns of the Colonial District's British-built lofty cathedral and cluster of public buildings – most famously *Raffles Hotel* – recalls the early days of British rule, when the area was the nucleus of Singapore.

▼ River taixs

▼ Old Parliament House

### The Singapore River

The spruced-up bank-side shop houses here comprise Singapore's most fashionable alfresco drinking and dining destination.

### Chinatown

Chinatown's gridded streets yield gilt altars, chanting monks, and traditional customs, trades, crafts and foodstuffs; bustling for most of the year, it really comes alive during Chinese New Year.

### Orchard Road

Think Bond Street, think Fifth Avenue, think Champs-Elysées: there are enough shopping centres and famous brands along this metropolis of retail malls to test even the most confirmed shopaholic.

▼ Worshipper at Thian Hock Keng Temple, Chinatown

## Central Business District

The monolithic towers of the CBD cast long shadows over the city. Stand in Raffles Place and look up at the skyline for long enough, and you'll swear Singapore's immaculate skyscrapers are bowing towards one another to form a roof above you.

▲ Sultan Mosque, Arab Quarter

## Little India

A sensual overload of gaudy Hindu temples, colourful sarees, aromatic spice stores, fortune-telling parrots and jasmine garlands.

▲ Flower garlands, Little India

## Arab Quarter

Singapore's Islamic heartland, where you can eat superb curries and breads and browse stores stacked with fine cloths and silks, as the Sultan Mosque muezzin's wailing call to prayer floats hauntingly on the warm evening air.

## Northern Singapore

Singapore's north-central heartland is home to the splendid Zoological Gardens, Night Safari and Bukit Timah Reserve, an incongruous but pristine pocket of primary rainforest.

# Ideas

# The Big Six

Part of the fun of visiting Singapore lies in taking in the eateries, markets and places of worship offered up by its diverse ethnic districts. But the island harbours several landmark tourist attractions that you really must not miss. Together, they reflect history, nature, ethnic culture and cuisine – in other words, all that's great about Singapore.

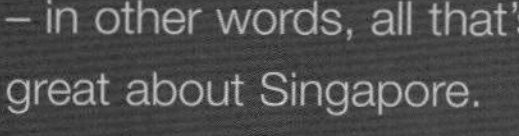

## ▲ Changi Museum

There's no more thought-provoking place on the island than this moving record of life for Singapore's World War II POWs.

P.123 ▸ Eastern Singapore

## ▲ Newton Circus Hawker Centre

Diners flock to this quintessential Singapore hawker centre, where Chinese, Indian and Malay stalls stand cheek by jowl.

P.79 ▸ Orchard Road and around

## ▲ Jurong BirdPark

You needn't be an ornithologist to get a real buzz from viewing the host of beautiful birds that are kept here in aviaries that mimic their residents' natural habitats.

P.134 ▸ Western Singapore

## ▲ National Museum

This beautiful example of colonial architecture is a worthy home for many of Singapore's greatest historical and cultural treasures.

P.70 ▸ Fort Canning Park and the western quays

## ▲ The Chinatown Heritage Centre

This ingeniously designed centre creates a true portrait of life in old Chinatown – complete with opium dens, Fifties' Chinese crooners and clan associations.

P.89 ▸ Chinatown

## ▼ Singapore Zoological Gardens

Its "open concept" – animals are contained by moats and glass, not bars – makes this as humane a zoo as you'll see.

P.117 ▸ Northern Singapore

# Iconic Singapore

Every great city has its defining images, and Singapore is no different. The colonial past figures heavily amongst these, and a number of icons pay homage to the state's colonial founder, Sir Stamford Raffles. If the Merlion nods to the island's historic links with the sea, then the magnificent, state-of-the art Theatres on the Bay complex has given the island a modern edifice to be proud of. And in the Singapore Sling, the city has given the world one of its classic cocktails.

## ▲ Sir Stamford Raffles

A formidable statue of the man marks the spot where Singapore's founder stepped ashore in 1819.

P.53 › Around the Padang

## ▲ Theatres on the Bay

This gob-smacking piece of contemporary design has transformed the downtown landscape.

P.55 › Around the Padang

## ▼ Singapore Sling

No trip to Singapore is complete without a glass of its signature cocktail – best tippled at *Raffles Hotel*.

P.58 ▸ Raffles Hotel and the northern Colonial District

## ▼ Raffles Hotel

Its affectionate soubriquet, the "grand old lady of the east", points to the personality and heritage of this legendary hotel.

P.58 ▸ Raffles Hotel and the northern Colonial District

## ▲ The Merlion

Singapore's ugly national symbol, half lion, half fish, stands defiantly at the mouth of the river.

P.97 ▸ The CBD and Boat Quay

# Animal kingdom

By any standards, Singapore's selection of attractions showcasing the natural world is impressive. Whether your particular focus of interest lies in the skies, on land or underwater, your imagination is sure to be sparked. You'll rarely find yourself peering through bars at Singapore's wildlife, either: the zoo, the bird park and Underwater World all boast state-of-the-art enclosures that afford you the unique privilege of walking among their residents.

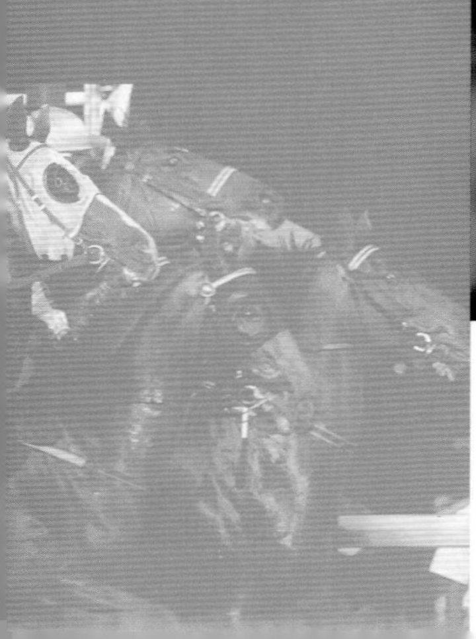

### ▲ Underwater World

The sensation of walking amongst sharks and rays is as exhilarating as it is disorienting.

P.138 ▸ Sentosa

### ▲ Night Safari

When the sun goes down, the animals wake up: a thousand nocturnal animals prowl this, the world's first wildlife park built for visits at night.

P.118 ▸ Northern Singapore

## ▶ Jurong BirdPark

This wonderful sanctuary makes unlikely neighbours of Antarctic penguins, New Zealand kiwis and Asian hornbills.

P.134 › Western Singapore

## ▼ Singapore Zoological Gardens

Singapore's zoo has won plaudits across the world for the humane and educative way it keeps and displays its awe-inspiring collection of creatures.

P.117 › Northern Singapore

## ◀ Singapore Turf Club

The rumble of hooves on a sultry tropical night is one of Singapore's great joys: the Lion City Cup, Singapore Gold Cup and Derby are the year's three biggest meets.

P.163 › Essentials

# Colonial Singapore

Singapore may have gained full independence in 1965, but its architecture and street names still nod to its colonial history. Take a trip along the streets of the downtown area – like the British, Singaporeans drive on the left – and you'll pass the churches and administrative buildings of colonial rule. Increasingly, these are morphing into arts centres, hotels and museums, ensuring that their impressive colonnaded facades are preserved for future generations.

### ▲ St Andrew's Cathedral

The walls shine bright at this nineteenth-century cathedral – Indian convict labour used coconut husks, eggs, lime and sugar to plaster them.

P.55 ▸ Around the Padang

### ▲ City Hall

Corinthian columns rise grandly above a sweeping central staircase, lending this building a stately feel.

P.55 ▸ Around the Padang

### ▶ Raffles Hotel

Stay at this legendary address, popular with generations of authors, and you might bag a room used by Somerset Maugham or Rudyard Kipling.

P.58 ▸ Raffles Hotel and northern Colonial District

### ◀ Singapore Cricket Club

A little outpost of Lord's in Southeast Asia; when viewed from across the Padang, this ochre-roofed colonial villa is nowadays dwarfed by the skyscrapers of Raffles Place.

P.54 ▸ Around the Padang

### ▼ Victoria Concert Hall and Theatre

Take in a play or performance, then pop round to Boat Quay for a late supper.

P.52 ▸ Around the Padang

# Singapore dining

Singaporeans live to eat, and thousands of restaurants and food stalls allow them to indulge their obsession. Since the city was built upon migration, there is no truly indigenous Singaporean cuisine, but residents have taken dishes such as Hainanese chicken rice, satay, chilli crab and fish-head curry to their hearts, and all stake a claim to national dish status. These days, Singapore can boast design-led gourmet restaurants to match anything London, Paris or New York has to offer; but for the quintessential dining experience, you'll want to head for a hot and smoky hawker centre.

▲ **Hawker stalls**

Fast food, Singapore-style – at hawker centres, such as *Maxwell Food Centre* in Chinatown, you find a table, and then choose dishes from the score of stalls around you.

P.93 ▸ Chinatown

▲ **Dim sum**

Head for restaurants such as *Mouth* in Chinatown to sample this breakfast- and lunchtime spread of dumplings and other tasty morsels.

P.93 ▸ Chinatown

## ▶ Chilli crab

You'll need plenty of paper napkins handy to negotiate a messy feast of pepper or chilli crab. At the *East Coast Seafood Centre*, you eat alfresco, overlooking the sea.

P.127 ▸ Eastern Singapore

## ◀ Murtabak

The venerable restaurants of North Bridge Road are the best places to see this popular Indian mince-and-onion pancake assembled and griddle-cooked.

P.112 ▸ The Arab Quarter

## ▶ Fish-head curry

It may stare disconcertingly back at you as you dine but fish-head curry is a wonderfully rich, hot and sour dish.

P.105 ▸ Little India

## ◀ Satay

Watching the satay man fan his coal fire with palm leaves at Lau Pa Sat Festival Market is pure culinary theatre.

P.92 ▸ Chinatown

# Religious landmarks

Few other places of its size in the world have as much religious diversity as Singapore. The faiths of the Chinese, Malays, Europeans and Indians that make up the Singaporean population have informed the community since its first days, leaving the island liberally sprinkled with temples, churches, mosques, *gurdwaras* and synagogues. All welcome visitors, though be sure to pay heed to any signs detailing worship times and dress codes, at the entrance.

## ▲ St Andrew's Cathedral

The surrounding skyscrapers and shopping malls have failed to dent the impact of this high-vaulted epicentre of the island's Christian faith.

P.55 ▸ Around the Padang

## ▲ The Sultan Mosque

During Muslim festivals, worshippers flock to Singapore's pre-eminent Islamic place of worship, whose golden dome and bristling steeples provide the Arab Quarter with its defining image.

P.107 ▸ The Arab Quarter

## ▶ Sri Mariamman Hindu Temple

The walls and roofs of the Indian community's Chinatown outpost teem with brightly painted statues of animals and deities.

P.86 ▸ Chinatown

## ▼ Armenian Church

This unfussy but charismatic building, named in full the Church of St Gregory the Illuminator, dates back to 1835.

P.69 ▸ Fort Canning Park and the western quays

## ▼ Thian Hock Keng Temple

The Chinese have worshipped on this site ever since early settlers burnt joss here to celebrate their safe passage.

P.81 ▸ Chinatown

## ▼ Sakaya Muni Buddha Gaya Temple

This remarkable Thai-built temple features a three-hundred-ton Buddha ringed by a thousand lights.

P.104 ▸ Little India

# Parks and gardens

Heavily urbanized and industrialized it may be, but Singapore still retains some verdant pockets. Indeed, even as you make your way into town from the airport, you'll be struck by the lushness of its landscape. But to experience Singapore's most beautiful scenery, you'll want to head for one of its dedicated spaces, where centuries-old trees tower over tropical blooms, and palm trees shade pristine beaches.

## ▲ Chinese Garden

Wander amongst the pagodas and bridges so typical of Chinese landscaping – or just lie down and relax on the peaceful lawns.

P.133 ▸ Western Singapore

## ▼ Mandai Orchid Gardens

With hillside terraces bursting with fabulously hued plants, this is as colourful a spot as you'll find in Singapore.

P.118 ▸ Northern Singapore

## ▲ Fort Canning Park

This erstwhile hub of colonial life boasts pleasing walks, great views and fascinating colonial relics.

P.68 ▸ Fort Canning Park and the western quays

## ▲ Singapore Botanic Gardens

Wandering the peaceful groves and lawns of the Botanic Gardens, you'll feel a million miles from the bustle of nearby Orchard Road.

P.76 ▸ Orchard Road and around

## ▼ East Coast Park

Not just kilometre after kilometre of clean, white sand – there are plenty of opportunities for watersports enthusiasts and some fine seafood restaurants, too.

P.123 ▸ Eastern Singapore

# Out on the town

The last decade has witnessed a huge evolution of the Singapore bar and club scene, meaning that a night's carousing no longer revolves around staid or tacky hotel venues. Whether you prefer to relax at a venerable colonial-style watering hole, or to don your dancing shoes for a night in a club, you're sure to find a joint to suit you.

### ▲ Zouk

Set within a one-time riverside godown, this standard-bearer of the Singapore clubbing scene has three themed clubs.

P.73 ▸ Fort Canning Park and the western quays

### ▲ City Space

Singapore has great views and great bars – and the two combine to spectacular effect here.

P.57 ▸ Around the Padang

## ▲ Crazy Elephant

There's something likeably rock'n'roll about this live music bar in Clarke Quay.

P.71 ▸ Fort Canning Park and the western quays

## ▲ Raffles Long Bar

With its dark wooden furnishings, rattan chairs and palm fans, this place has the feel of a nineteenth-century plantation building.

P.64 ▸ Raffles Hotel and the northern Colonial District

## ▲ Ministry of Sound

Don't miss this recent addition to the world's number one clubbing portfolio.

P.73 ▸ Fort Canning Park and the western quays

## ▼ Boat Quay

This pretty stretch of converted shophouses has transformed itself into the island's most happening place to eat and drink.

P.97 ▸ The CBD and Boat Quay

# Wartime Singapore

Memories abound of Singapore's invasion and occupation by the Japanese during the latter part of World War II, and no wonder: tens of thousands of Allied soldiers and locals lost their lives between 1942 and 1945. Sites recalling these dark times fall into two types: those that tell the moving stories of the individuals and communities that were affected by the conflict; and those that allow you to experience the harrowing sights, sounds and hardware of war for yourself.

## ▲ Memories at Old Ford Factory

This compelling account of life under Japanese rule during World War II is, fittingly, housed on the site of the Allied surrender in 1942.

P.115 ▸ Northern Singapore

## ▲ Changi Museum

The messages left by relatives at this humbling museum prove that, for many, the impact of the War lives on.

P.123 ▸ Eastern Singapore

## ▲ Fort Siloso

Colonial folly embodied: these south-facing guns couldn't avert a Japanese offensive from the north.

P.142 ▸ Sentosa

## ▼ The Battle Box

Visitors descend into the bowels of Fort Canning Hill to visit the bunkers of Allied Command.

P.68 ▸ Fort Canning Park and the western quays

## ◀ Kranji War Cemetery and Memorial

Not even the hardest heart could remain unmoved by this testament to the enormous loss of life Singapore witnessed in the War.

P.119 ▸ Northern Singapore

# Kids' Singapore

With its wartime tunnels and fortune-telling parrots, deities and dragons, monkeys and penguins, Singapore has plenty to amuse young visitors. And, while exploring the city's various districts unearths sights and sounds galore to stoke young imaginations, the island also has numerous attractions aimed more explicitly at kids – several of which carry an educational subtext.

### ▲ Sentosa Luge

Whiz down the lengthy slope on a toboggan-cum-go-cart, take a chairlift to the top, and do it again.

P.142 ▸ Sentosa

## ▼ Singapore DuckTours

Is it a bus? Is it a boat? This land-and-sea experience guarantees a unique tour of Singapore.

P.159 ▸ Essentials

## ▼ Singapore Science Centre

Packed with multimedia exhibits and interactive displays, there's much to learn here as well as plenty of fun to be had.

P.133 ▸ Western Singapore

## ▲ Haw Par Villa

Giant dragons, grisly scenes from hell and fantastic journeys with magical characters from legend – what more could a child ask of a statue park?

P.130 ▸ Western Singapore

## ▼ Singapore Zoological Gardens

Kids will relish the chance to have a picture taken with a sea lion, or to have breakfast with an orang-utan.

P.117 ▸ Northern Singapore

# Shops & markets

The Singaporean love affair with shopping has spawned a giddying range of outlets and products. In the gleaming shopping malls of Orchard Road, you'll find boutiques and department stores selling everything from pricey antiques to the sharpest designer brands. At the other end of the price scale, Singapore's markets offer an appealing taster of city life. If you're happy to haggle, head for the ethnic enclaves, where you can take your pick of handcrafted textiles, jewellery, artefacts and all sorts of knick-knacks.

### ▲ Eu Yan Sang Medical Hall

The use of roots and herbs – and centipedes and gall bladders – in traditional Chinese medicine is best demonstrated at Chinatown's Eu Yan Sang shop.

P.85 ▸ Chinatown

### ▲ Arab Street

Don't expect to find a price tag on the lustrous silks and batiks on display here – half the fun is in the negotiation.

P.108 ▸ The Arab Quarter

## ▶ Antique shops

Orchard Road's Tanglin district yields books, statues and artworks reflecting all the component cultures of melting-pot Singapore.

P.77 ▸ Orchard Road and around

## ▼ Wet markets

Goats' heads, gutted fish, animal carcasses – Singapore's wet markets are not for the faint-hearted.

P.90 ▸ Chinatown

## ▲ Tekka Market

Indian textiles, sarees and sandals make a good gift or souvenir – this busy market always has an excellent selection.

P.102 ▸ Little India

## ◀ Sim Lim Square

Haggle hard and you'll be able to pick up a bargain at this electronics and IT emporium.

P.63 ▸ Raffles Hotel and the northern Colonial District

# Wild Singapore

Singapore's protected green spaces recall a time when the entire island was blanketed by primary rainforest and ringed by mangrove swampland. There's plenty of scope for exploring the natural world here, and you'll be surprised by the comprehensiveness of the island's hiking trail network. Meanwhile, a twenty-minute boat trip from Changi Point, in the far east of the island, takes you to Pulau Ubin, whose dirt tracks and stilt house hamlets act as a sort of Singaporean time capsule.

## ▲ Sungei Buloh Wetland Reserve

A last refuge for the mangrove swamp that dominated the island's waterline when Raffles stepped ashore in 1819.

P.120 ▸ Northern Singapore

## ▲ HSBC TreeTop Walk

This suspended nature walk provides first-hand experience of the forest canopy.

P.116 ▸ Northern Singapore

## ▲ Bukit Timah Nature Reserve

The macaques here are as wild as the primary forest they inhabit – get too close and you might get a nip from them.

P.113 ▸ Northern Singapore

## ▶ Pulau Ubin

Locals say this sleepy island gives an authentic picture of what the east coast of Singapore was like fifty years ago.

P.124 ▸ Eastern Singapore

## ▼ MacRitchie Trails

There are kilometre upon kilometre of nature trails here, just a twenty-minute taxi ride from downtown Singapore.

P.116 ▸ Northern Singapore

# Multicultural Singapore

All corners of Asia meet in multicultural Singapore: in the space of a couple of hours, you could tuck into a south Indian curry served on a banana leaf, browse for silks and linens in an Arab Quarter textile store, and pop into a Buddhist temple to watch worshippers offer up incense to their ancestors. Local tour guide firms will whisk you from one ethnic enclave to another; but in truth there's no better way to soak up the atmosphere than to stroll around independently.

### ▲ Hindu temples

As long as you slip off your shoes, you are welcome to explore the daily rituals and fantastical statues at Singapore's Hindu temples, such as Sri Veeramakaliamman Temple in Little India.

P.103 ▸ Little India

## ▶ Arab Quarter

This downtown district is the spiritual heart of Singapore's Muslim community, and home to some cracking restaurants.

P.107 ▸ The Arab Quarter

## ◀ Chinatown

Singapore's most extensive ethnic enclave moves with the times, but the old ways live on at addresses like Sian Chai Kang Temple.

P.84 ▸ Chinatown

## ▼ Chinese opera

Grab the opportunity to witness the highly stylized sights and sounds of a *wayang* while you are in town. The best time to catch one is during the Festival of the Hungry Ghosts.

P.161 ▸ Essentials

## ▲ Little India

The city's Indian district is characterized by colourful temples, lip-smacking curries and idiosyncratic personalities.

P.100 ▸ Little India

# Museums

The existence of a number of fascinating specialist collections adds to the extraordinary diversity of attractions around Singapore. There are museums dedicated to subjects as varied as Chinese immigrants, fire-fighting, World War II and Asian arts and culture. But far and away the most compelling is the National Museum, whose collection has been constructed around its eleven "treasures", among them a fragment of the mysterious Singapore Stone, which once guarded the mouth of the Singapore River.

## ▲ Civil Defence Heritage Galleries

Within a colonial-era fire station, this engaging attraction encompasses fire-fighting equipment, ancient and modern, and much more besides.

P.69 ▸ Fort Canning and the western quays

## ▲ The Chinatown Heritage Centre

The reconstruction of the squalid living quarters endured by early Chinese coolies is one of the highlights of this excellent centre.

P.89 ▸ Chinatown

## ▶ Singapore Art Museum

The thoughtful juxtaposition of Asian and Western artworks ensures there's something to suit all tastes.

P.61 ▸ Raffles Hotel and the northern Colonial District

## ▲ National Museum

Packed with exhibits, the National Museum's Singapore History Gallery relates the story of this small but influential island, from the fourteenth century up to the present day.

P.70 ▸ Fort Canning Park and the western quays

## ▼ Asian Civilisations Museum

Set in a splendid Neoclassical building, this museum is a one-stop shop for lovers of Asian culture, religion and history.

P.51 ▸ Around the Padang

# Drama and the arts

Long something of a cultural desert, Singapore has in recent times witnessed a burgeoning arts scene that reflects the government's intention to become the region's cultural capital. Since the opening of the Theatres on the Bay complex early in the new millennium, the artistic scene hasn't looked back, and these days you can catch music, drama and film at a broad range of venues across the city. There's an expanding roster of high-profile arts festivals, too.

### ▲ Classical music

There's no more grandiose classical music venue than the Victoria Concert Hall.

P.52 ▸ Around the Padang

### ▲ WOMAD

It's no surprise that so multicultural a community as Singapore should embrace the global arts scene every year.

P.161 ▸ Essentials

## ▶ Esplanade – Theatres on the Bay

Its futuristic exterior divides local opinion, but its diverse programme of events draws universal acclaim.

P.55 ▸ Around the Padang

## ▼ Cinema

Take in an Asian movie; the subtitles will help you keep up with the plot.

P.162 ▸ Essentials

## ▲ Chinese opera

At the *Chinese Opera Teahouse*, you can enjoy a Chinese dinner while classically trained singers perform for you.

P.92 ▸ Chinatown

# Active Singapore

It's easy to overindulge in food-crazy Singapore, so it's happy news that there are oodles of ways to get active and work off that last bowl of noodles. Singapore and its main islands, Ubin and Sentosa, offer endless opportunities for exertion – whether you favour cycling or rollerblading, trekking or swimming, golfing or windsurfing. If you are out in the sun, though, don't forget to slip, slap, slop.

▲ **Rollerblading**

The long, arrow-straight paths of East Coast Park are ideal for rollerbladers, as well as cyclists.

P.123 ▸ Eastern Singapore

▲ **Golf**

There are several truly world-class courses on the island, though some of them aren't cheap. If you're less serious about the game, head for Sijori WonderGolf on Sentosa (p.143).

P.162 ▸ Essentials

## ▶ Swimming

The waters around Singapore are kept very clean – on Sentosa, handily placed bars mean you can wallow in the warm waters, then grab a cooling beer.

P.143 ▸ Sentosa

## ▼ Windsurfing

Sea-locked Singapore has numerous watersports operators. Windsurfing, sailing and water-skiing are all possible, particularly off the east coast.

P.163 ▸ Essentials

## ▲ Cycling

The busy roads downtown are best avoided, but pedalling around outlying areas, such as Ubin or East Coast Park, is huge fun.

P.158 ▸ Essentials

# Stay in style

Whether you prefer the classic ambience of a bygone era or the stylish interiors and state-of-the-art gizmos of a brand new hotel, Singapore has places to stay that can pamper with the best of them. Soaring twenty-first-century towers stand cheek by jowl with century-old colonial piles; all share top-notch standards of service, and are out to impress with their spas, pools and design. For real character, opt for one of the new brand of style-led boutique hotels that's transforming the Chinatown accommodation scene.

▲ **Goodwood Park Hotel**

This splendid colonial edifice was named a national monument in 1989.

P.151 ▸ Accommodation

▲ **New Majestic Hotel**

Emerging Singaporean artists were invited to design the rooms at this classy boutique hotel – eclectic, modern and fab.

P.152 ▸ Accommodation

## Fullerton Hotel

The infinity pool at this sumptuous hotel, carved out of the former GPO, offers peerless views of Boat Quay.

P.153 ▸ Accommodation

## Raffles Hotel

When all is said and done, the defining Singaporean hotel experience still has to be *Raffles*, which has been boarding visitors to the island since 1887.

P.58 &150 ▸ Raffles Hotel and northern Colonial District

## Shangri-La Hotel

Customer service is often said to be the best in the world at the *Shangri-La*. Bougainvillea-fronted rooms in its garden wing overlook the tempting pool.

P.151 ▸ Accommodation

## Marina Mandarin Hotel

Even if you don't stay in one of its graceful rooms, it's well worth a visit just to stare up at its awe-inspiring central atrium.

P.150 ▸ Accommodation

# Singapore celebrates

Each of Singapore's distinct ethnic communities maintains a busy roster of traditional festivals and celebrations, meaning that, whenever you time your visit, you have a good chance of coinciding with some or other colourful event. From exuberant pageants that all the family can enjoy, to gory displays of devotion, all of Singapore's festivals are celebrated with great gusto, making them an ideal way to get to grips with a new culture.

### ▲ Thimithi

Every year, Hindu devotees run across hot coals to prove their faith at Chinatown's Sri Mariamman Temple.

P.87 ▸ Chinatown

### ▲ Dragon Boat Festival

Drums beat to keep rowers to time – think *Spartacus*, with an Asian slant.

P.161 ▸ Essentials

## ▶ Chinese New Year

Join the hordes in Chinatown for this, the biggest celebration in Singapore's calendar.

P.160 ▸ Essentials

## ◀ Mid-autumn Festival

Children parade with brightly coloured lanterns, and Chinatown shops stock up with seasonal mooncakes.

P.161 ▸ Essentials

## ▼ Christmas

Downtown shopping centres compete to create the most outlandish and impressive festive displays.

P.161 ▸ Essentials

## ▲ Thaipusam

Singapore goriest spectacle: devotees skewer their skin, cheeks and tongues as an act of penitence.

P.104 ▸ Little India

# Viewpoints

With its soaring skyscrapers, Singapore has plenty of vantage points from which you can enjoy vistas that will stop you dead in your tracks. From the upper floors of the *Swissôtel*, for example, you can clearly see as far as southern Malaysia and Indonesia's Riau Archipelago, while from Mount Faber, out west, or the cable car to Sentosa, there are stunning views back into the downtown district.

## ▲ The Swissôtel

Seventy floors up, and with ceiling-to-floor windows, the view from the bars at this towering hotel is not for the faint of heart.

P.57 ▸ Around the Padang

## ▲ Boat Quay

The lights of Singapore's coolest dining district twinkle at night, reflecting alluringly in the waters of the river.

P.97 ▸ The CBD and Boat Quay

### ▼ Cable Car to Sentosa

Head across to Sentosa at sunset and you can dine in one of the string of cars stretching from Mount Faber to the island.

P.138 ▸ Sentosa

### ▲ Mount Faber

The 360-degree views from this modest hill are outstanding – and there are bars on the summit, so you can enjoy them over a drink.

P.129 ▸ Western Singapore

### ◀ Raffles Place

An astonishing view from the ground up to the lofty pinnacles of Singapore's financial powerhouses.

P.95 ▸ The CBD and Boat Quay

金山寺

# Places

CapitaLand

# Around the Padang

**The beating heart of Singapore's Colonial District is the immaculately groomed Padang, whose grass is kept pristine by a bevy of gardeners on state-of-the-art lawnmowers. Once the focal point of colonial society and perambulation, the Padang ("field" in Malay) now plays host to cricket matches, rugby sevens tournaments and cultural festivals. When it lies fallow, focus falls on the stately, white-washed and colonnaded piles of nineteenth-century colonial rule – cathedral, court, concert hall, theatre, parliament building – that hem it. Of particular interest are the former government offices of the Empress Place Building, now a trove of Asian artworks and exhibits in the form of the Asian Civilisations Museum. The ultra-modern Theatres on the Bay complex and the new Sir Norman Foster-designed Supreme Court bring the area bang up-to-date. There are plenty of places to eat and drink in the area, with steepling Raffles City offering the greatest breadth of shopping, as well as the most breathtaking views of the island.**

## Asian Civilisations Museum

Empress Place ⓣ63327798, ⓦwww.nhb.gov.sg/acm. Mon 1–7pm, Tues–Thurs, Sat & Sun 9am–7pm, Fri 9am–9pm. $5, including free guided tour (Mon 2pm, Tues–Fri 11am & 2pm, Sat & Sun 11am, 2pm & 3.30pm).

Empress Place Building, a robust Neoclassical structure named after Queen Victoria and completed in 1865, houses the Asian Civilisations Museum, which traces the origins and growth of Asia's many and varied cultures. Its ten themed galleries hold over a thousand artefacts and bring to life the religions, history and cultures of every corner of Asia. One gallery showcases Southeast Asian musical instruments, puppetry and jewellery, while another is devoted to ancient Indian

▲ GARDENER ON THE PADANG

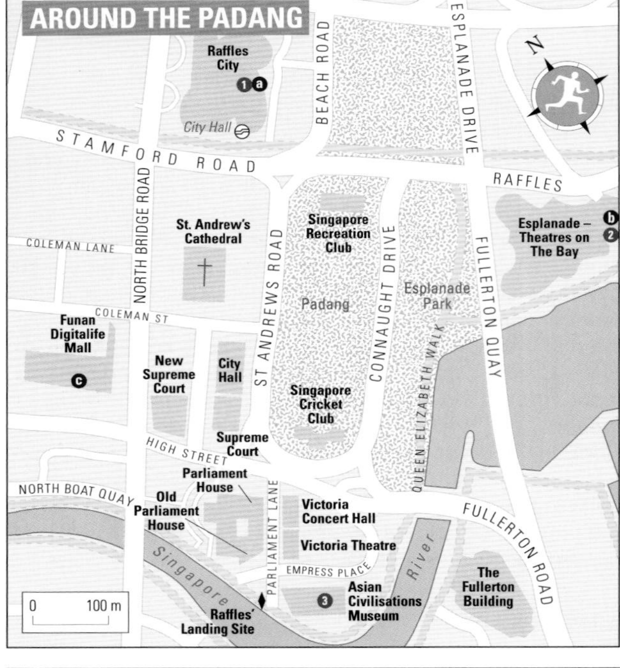


| EATING | | BARS | | SHOPS | | | |
|---|---|---|---|---|---|---|---|
| Colours by the Bay | 2 | Bar Opiume | 3 | China Mec | a | Selangor Pewter | a |
| Indochine Waterfront | 3 | City Space | 1 | Kinokuniya | a | Tatami Shop | b |
| | | | | Roxy Records | c | | |

paintings, textiles and stone sculptures. Artwork, calligraphic tools and projected images of mosques from around the world are featured at the West Asian/ Islamic Gallery. Temporary exhibitions allow visitors to drill down further into specific facets of Asian life and culture – recent exhibitions have focused on Japanese masks, Asia's nomadic tribes and Chinese royal textiles. The museum's Singapore River Interpretive Gallery features recorded oral accounts of life along the river delivered by individuals that lived beside it and worked it all their lives.

## Victoria Concert Hall and Theatre

Empress Place. With their colonnaded facades and stucco garlands, the Victoria Concert Hall and adjoining Victoria Theatre are both fine examples of colonial architecture. The theatre was completed in 1862 as Singapore's town hall, while the concert hall was added in 1905 as a memorial to Queen Victoria's reign; both remain the venues for some of Singapore's most prestigious cultural events (see p.162). During the Japanese occupation, the concert hall's clock tower was altered to

## Sir Stamford Raffles

Fittingly for a man who would spend his life roaming the globe, the founder of modern Singapore, **Sir Stamford Raffles**, was born at sea, in 1781. A decade of diligent work as a clerk for the **East India Company** in London won him a passage to Penang in 1805. Once in Southeast Asia, his rise was meteoric: by 1811 he was Governor of Java, where his rule was regarded as wise, libertarian and compassionate, and he introduced much-needed reforms. Another governorship post followed on the southern coast of Sumatra, where he also found time to study the flora and fauna tirelessly – he discovered the huge *Rafflesia arnoldi* on a field trip. In 1819, with British interests in the area under threat from the Dutch, Raffles was given leave to establish a British base in the Straits of Melaka, and in 1819 he duly sailed to the southern tip of the Malay Peninsula, where his securing of Singapore from its Malay rulers was a daring masterstroke of diplomacy.

For a man so inextricably linked with Singapore, Raffles spent scant time on the island. His first stay was for one week, the second for three weeks, during which time he helped delineate the new settlement. He visited Singapore one last time in 1822. By August 1824, Raffles was back in England, where he spent his free time founding London Zoo and setting up a farm in Hendon. By now he was dogged by ill health and financial difficulties, and he died in 1826 from a brain tumour. A friend of William Wilberforce, Raffles is commemorated by a statue in Westminster Abbey.

Tokyo time, while the statue of Raffles that once stood in front of it narrowly escaped being melted down; after its near-miss it was sent to the National Museum, where the newly installed Japanese curator hid it and reported it destroyed. A copy can be seen down Parliament Lane by the river at Raffles' landing site, where, in January 1819, the great man apparently took his first steps on Singaporean soil.

### The Parliament buildings

Parliament Lane. To view sessions in Parliament House, call ⓣ63326666 or check ⓦwww.parliament.gov.sg. The dignified, white Victorian building ringed by fencing is the Old Parliament House, built by Singapore's pre-eminent colonial architect, Irishman George Drumgould Coleman. Relieved of its legislative duties, the building is now known as the Arts House and is home to cafés, shops, galleries and a film

▲ CLOCKTOWER, VICTORIA CONCERT HALL

▲ ELEPHANT STATUE OUTSIDE OLD PARLIAMENT HOUSE

and theatre space which displays works by local artists. The bronze elephant in front of the Old Parliament House was a gift to Singapore from King Rama V of Thailand (whose father was the king upon whom *The King and I* was based) after his trip to the island in 1871 – the first foreign visit ever made by a Thai monarch. It is sometimes possible to watch Singapore's parliament in session in the new Parliament House, across Parliament Lane from its predecessor.

## Singapore Cricket Club

Connaught Drive. The brown-tiled roof, whitewashed walls and dark-green blinds of the Singapore Cricket Club, on the southern skirts of the Padang, have a nostalgic charm. Founded in the 1850s, the clubhouse was the hub of colonial British society and still operates a "members only" rule at all times, though there's nothing to stop you watching the action from outside on the Padang itself. As well as cricket, a plethora of other big sporting events, including the Singapore Rugby Sevens, are played out on the Padang, and there are frequent parades; a timetable of forthcoming events is available at the club's reception.

## The Supreme Court buildings

Constructed in Neoclassical style, Singapore's erstwhile Supreme Court, on St Andrew's Road, sports a domed roof of green lead and a splendid, wood-panelled entrance hall. When it was built in the 1930s, the building replaced the exclusive *Hotel de L'Europe*, whose drawing rooms allegedly provided author and playwright Somerset Maugham with inspiration for many of his Southeast Asia short stories. Since early in the millennium, the building has sat idle, awaiting a fresh purpose, but its replacement, the Sir Norman

▲ NEW SUPREME COURT

Foster-designed New Supreme Court, a block back on North Bridge Road, is also worthy of note – though more for its impressive, flying saucer-shaped upper tier than for its lumpen marble and glass main body.

### City Hall

St Andrew's Rd. City Hall's uniform rows of grandiose Corinthian columns lend it the austere air of a mausoleum. It was on the steps here that Lord Louis Mountbatten, then Supreme Allied Commander in Southeast Asia, announced Japan's surrender to the British in 1945. Fourteen years later, modern Singapore's political godfather, Lee Kuan Yew, chose the same spot from which to address his electorate at a victory rally celebrating self-government for Singapore. The steps witness less dramatic events today, as newlyweds line up to have their big day captured in front of one of Singapore's most imposing buildings. Like the old Supreme Court, City Hall currently lies empty, pending reinvention.

### St Andrew's Cathedral

At the junction of Coleman St and North Bridge Road. St Andrew's Cathedral gleams even brighter than the other fruits of grandiose empire-building around the Padang. Consecrated in 1862, the cathedral was constructed in high-vaulted, Neo-Gothic style, using Indian convict labour. Its exterior walls were plastered using Madras *chunam* (a composite of eggs, lime, sugar and shredded coconut husks which shines brightly when smoothed) while the small cross behind the pulpit was crafted from two fourteenth-century nails salvaged from the ruins of Coventry Cathedral in England, which was destroyed during World War II. During the Japanese invasion of Singapore, the cathedral became a makeshift hospital; the vestry was an operating theatre and the nave a ward.

### Esplanade – Theatres on the Bay

Ⓦwww.esplanade.com. Guided tours Mon–Fri 11am & 2pm, Sat & Sun 11am; $8; Ⓣ68288377; meet at the Concourse Information Counter. No other Singaporean building has caused as many ripples as the $600-million Esplanade – Theatres on the Bay project, which occupies six hectares of waterfront land east of the Padang. Opinion is split over whether the two huge, spiked shells that roof the complex are peerless modernistic architecture or indulgent kitsch. Locals have taken to calling them "the durians" after the spiky and pungent fruit, and they have also been variously compared to hedgehogs, kitchen sieves, golf balls, huge microphones, and even mating aardvarks; perhaps the greatest likeness, though, is to two giant insects' eyes. Esplanade boasts a concert hall, theatre, recital studio, theatre studio, gallery space and outdoor theatre (see also p.162), all of which you'll take in on the guided tour of the complex. Around the building threads Esplanade Mall, offering places to shop, eat and drink – on the southern side of the complex there are peerless views across the bay.

### Raffles City

Looming large at the junction of Beach Road and Stamford Road, the huge Raffles City development was designed by Chinese-American architect I.M. Pei, the man behind the Louvre's glass pyramid, and completed in

1985. It comprises two enormous hotels, a multi-level shopping centre and floor upon floor of offices and hotel rooms, one of which, the *Swissôtel*, holds an annual vertical marathon in November. Hardy athletes attempt to run up to the top floor in as short a time as possible: the current record stands at under seven minutes.

## Shops

### China Mec

03-31/32 Raffles City Shopping Centre, 252 North Bridge Rd. There's a vast selection of handcrafted cloisonné goods – patterned bowls, teapots, statues, jars and other articles decorated with copper inlays and enamel – available at this beautiful shop.

### Kinokuniya

Sogo Department Store, 3rd floor, Raffles City Shopping Centre, 250 North Bridge Rd. While not as big as the flagship branch on Orchard Road, this eminently browsable bookstore caters to all tastes, from Western to Asian, and from Dan Brown to Daniel Defoe.

### Roxy Records

03-36 Funan Digitalife Mall, 109 North Bridge Rd. Roxy is a well established and discerning CD store offering a good collection of indie and dance sounds. It also carries a healthy stock of work by Singaporean artists.

### Selangor Pewter

03-33 Raffles City Shopping Centre, 252 North Bridge Rd. Royal Selangor has been crafting from tin, copper and antimony for well over a century. At this showroom, you'll find a range of products from tankards to vases, and from photo frames to desk accessories.

### Tatami Shop

02-10 Esplanade Mall, 8 Raffles Ave. This is a charming shop within the Theatres on the Bay, specializing in Japanese tatami mats, rugs and miscellanea.

▼ ESPLANADE – THEATRES ON THE BAY

# Eating

## Colours by the Bay

Esplanade Mall, 8 Raffles Ave. Restaurant collective, offering a number of global cuisines – Japanese, Thai, Chinese, Italian – overlooking the bay beside Singapore's main theatre. With luck, your meal will coincide with an alfresco cultural performance of music and dance. Two can dine well for $15.

## Indochine Waterfront

Asian Civilisations Museum, 1 Empress Place ☎63391720. Closed lunchtime Sat & Sun. The exquisite Southeast Asian dining here is a class apart, and the decor – crystal chandeliers, tall Buddha statues and Ming-style chairs – breathtaking. Tuck into Cambodian chilli and basil chicken ($20), or perhaps the sesame lamb tenderloin with lemongrass ($32). For dessert, give the more exotic fare a miss, and order the melt in the mouth banana fritters.

▲ COCKTAILS AT *CITY SPACE*

# Bars

## Bar Opiume

Asian Civilisations Museum, 1 Empress Place. Mon–Thurs 5pm–2am, Fri & Sat 5pm–3am. Cool-as-ice cocktail bar, where the barmen mix a mean Singapore Sling. Outside are drop-dead gorgeous views of the waterfront; inside is a bar of mature sophistication, graced by huge crystal chandeliers, modish, square-cut leather furniture and a lordly standing Buddha statue.

## City Space

70th floor, *Swissôtel The Stamford*, 2 Stamford Rd. Mon–Thurs & Sun 5pm–1am, Fri & Sat 5pm–2am. Exquisitely appointed lounge bar – but decor be hanged: you come to *City Space* to drink in the peerless, seventy-storey views across Singapore to southern Malaysia. The cocktails aren't cheap, but the warmed chilli cashews that come with your drink are to die for.

▲ *BAR OPIUME*

# Raffles Hotel and the northern Colonial District

**In *Raffles Hotel*, Singapore boasts one of Asia's most iconic stones of Empire; its many legends prompted author and playwright Somerset Maugham to remark that it "stood for all the fables of the exotic East". A meal – or, at least, a Singapore Sling – at the hotel is *de rigueur* on a trip to Singapore. Once a beach-front property, today *Raffles* is besieged by the traffic and bustle of the northern Colonial District, whose dense but walkable grid of roads still bears street names such as Queen, Victoria, Albert and Waterloo – the latter drawing a mass of local worshippers to its Buddhist and Hindu temples. A short walk along teeming Bras Basah Road from *Raffles* lie Singapore's most attractive drinking and dining venue, CHIJMES, and the Singapore Art Museum, an illuminating collection of artworks on Asian culture, while the the east, vast Suntec City provides plenty of further scope for eating and drinking.**

## Raffles Hotel

1 Beach Rd. Raffles Museum open daily 10am–9pm. Free. (See also p.150). *Raffles Hotel* opened for business in 1887, when four Armenian brothers acquired a ten-room beach-front colonial bungalow at the junction of

▲ RAFFLES HOTEL

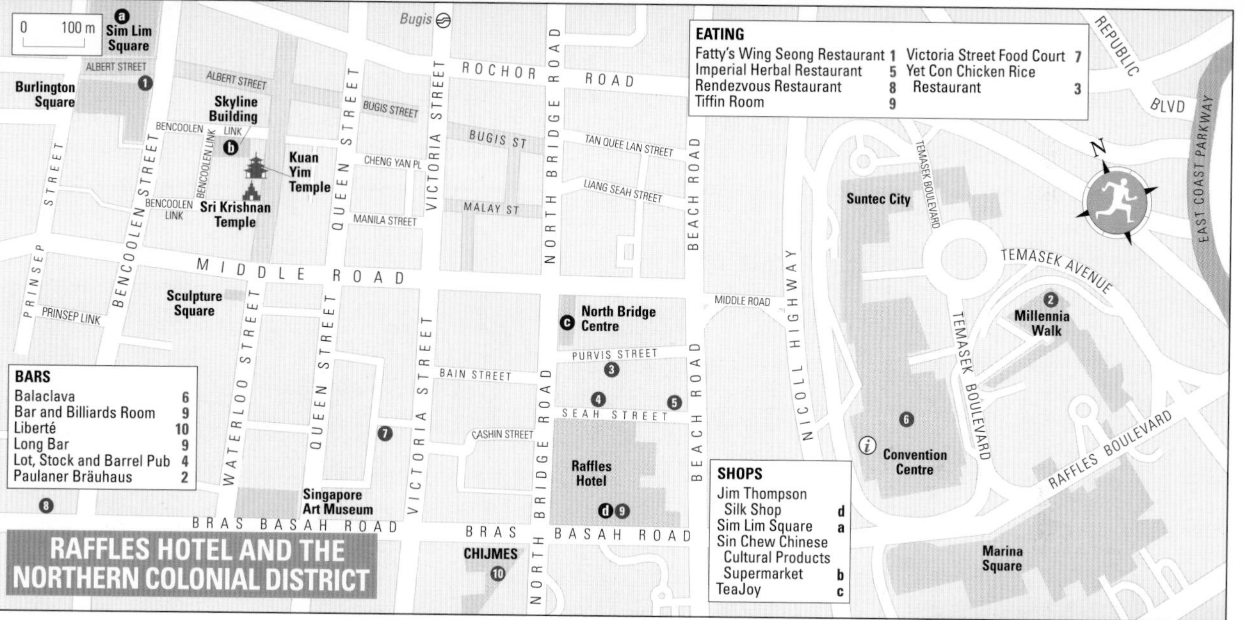
RAFFLES HOTEL AND THE NORTHERN COLONIAL DISTRICT
EATING
Fatty's Wing Seong Restaurant 1
Imperial Herbal Restaurant 5
Rendezvous Restaurant 8
Tiffin Room 9
Victoria Street Food Court 7
Yet Con Chicken Rice Restaurant 3
BARS
Balaclava 6
Bar and Billiards Room 9
Liberté 10
Long Bar 9
Lot, Stock and Barrel Pub 4
Paulaner Bräuhaus 2
SHOPS
Jim Thompson Silk Shop d
Sim Lim Square a
Sin Chew Chinese Cultural Products Supermarket b
TeaJoy c
0 100 m
Sim Lim Square
Burlington Square
Skyline Building
Kuan Yim Temple
Sri Krishnan Temple
Sculpture Square
Singapore Art Museum
CHIJMES
North Bridge Centre
Raffles Hotel
Suntec City
Convention Centre
Millennia Walk
Marina Square
Bugis
ALBERT STREET
BENCOOLEN LINK
BENCOOLEN STREET
PRINSEP STREET
PRINSEP LINK
MIDDLE ROAD
WATERLOO STREET
QUEEN STREET
BUGIS STREET
CHENG YAN PL
MANILA STREET
VICTORIA STREET
ROCHOR ROAD
BUGIS ST
MALAY ST
BAIN STREET
CASHIN STREET
NORTH BRIDGE ROAD
TAN QUEE LAN STREET
LIANG SEAH STREET
PURVIS STREET
SEAH STREET
BEACH ROAD
BRAS BASAH ROAD
NICOLL HIGHWAY
TEMASEK BOULEVARD
TEMASEK AVENUE
RAFFLES BOULEVARD
REPUBLIC BLVD
EAST COAST PARKWAY
N

Beach and Bras Basah roads. The brothers, who already owned Penang's *Eastern & Oriental Hotel*, set about augmenting their hotel with the lofty halls, restaurants, bars, ballroom and peaceful gardens that today's visitors enjoy. But it was not until the first three decades of the twentieth century, when it established its reputation for luxury and elegance – it was the first building in Singapore with electric lights and fans – that the hotel reached its heyday. In 1902, a piece of Singaporean history was made (though probably an apocryphal tale) when the last tiger to be killed on the island was shot inside the building. Thirteen years later another *Raffles* legend, the Singapore Sling cocktail, was created by bartender Ngiam Tong Boon. The rich, famous and influential have always patronized the hotel, but it is most proud of its literary connections. Herman Hesse, Somerset Maugham, Noël Coward and Günter Grass and, probably, Joseph Conrad all stayed at *Raffles* at some time – Maugham is said to have written many of his Asian tales under a frangipani tree in the garden. After World War II, the hotel entered a period of decline, and it remained little more than a shabby tourist diversion until a $160-million face-lift in 1991. While the hotel retains much of its colonial grace, the shopping arcade that curves around the back, selling *Raffles*-related souvenirs, exclusive garments, leatherware and perfume, lacks finesse. Still, if you're in Singapore, there's no missing *Raffles*.

Upstairs and at the back of the hotel complex, the Raffles Museum is crammed with memorabilia, much of which was recovered in a nationwide heritage search that encouraged Singaporeans to turn in china, silverware and other "souvenirs" that had found their way up sleeves and into handbags over the years.

▲ CHIJMES

## CHIJMES

Based around the Neo-Gothic husk of the former Convent of the Holy Infant Jesus (from whose name the complex's acronymic title is derived), CHIJMES has established itself as one of the island's premier eating and drinking venues over the past decade. Landscaped with lawns, courtyards, waterfalls, fountains and a

▲ SINGAPORE ART MUSEUM

sunken forecourt, the complex dates back to 1854, when four French nuns arrived in Singapore from Penang. A relic from its convent days survives on its Victoria Street flank, in the shape of the Gate of Hope, where local families left unwanted babies in order to be taken in. Many were "Tiger girls", so called because they were born in the Year of the Tiger and thus thought to bring bad luck to their families.

### Singapore Art Museum

71 Bras Basah Rd ⓣ63323222, ⓦwww.singart.com. Daily 10am–7pm, Fri till 9pm. $3, including free tour Mon 2pm, Tues–Thurs 11am & 2pm, Fri 11am, 2pm & 7pm, Sat & Sun 11am, 2pm & 3.30pm. Whether you have eclectic artistic tastes, or a more specific leaning towards regional Asian art, you'll find works to delight you at the Singapore Art Museum. Its rolling schedule of visiting collections has brought work by such acclaimed artists as Marc Chagall and the sculptor Carl Milles to Singapore. But greater emphasis is placed on contemporary local and Southeast Asian artists and artwork – indeed, the museum's real strength lies in its permanent collection's mapping of the Asian experience. Only a selection from the collection is displayed at any one time, but works you may be lucky enough to catch are Bui Xian Phai's *Coalmine*, an unremittingly desolate memory of his labour in a Vietnamese re-education camp, and Srihadi Sudarsono's *Horizon Dan Prahu*, in which traditional Indonesian fishing boats ply a Mark Rothko-esque canvas. Look out, too, for sketches and paintings by local artist, Liu Kang, of postwar kampung life in Singapore.

The museum enjoys a peerless location in the venerable St Joseph's Institution, Singapore's first Catholic school, whose silvery dome rang to the sounds of school bells and rote learning until 1987. Though extensions have been necessary, many of the school's original rooms survive, among them the school chapel (now an auditorium), whose Stations of the Cross and mosaic floor remain intact. The school quad, the former gymnasium, periodically displays statues and sculptures, such as the glassworks of American designer Dale Chihuly.

## Kuan Yim Temple and Waterloo Street

Thanks to an expansion and modernization project back in the 1980s, Kuan Yim Temple, named after the Buddhist goddess of mercy, may not have the cluttered altars, dusty old rafters and elaborate roofs of Chinatown's temples, but it nonetheless remains one of the most popular in Singapore to visit. Thousands of devotees flock here every day, and, all along the pavement outside on Waterloo Street, old ladies in floppy, wide-brimmed hats sell them fresh flowers from baskets. Religious artefact shops in the surrounding buildings are well placed to catch worshippers on their way out. One shop specializes in small shrines for the house – the de luxe model boasts flashing lights and an extractor fan to expel unwanted incense smoke. Fortune-tellers and street traders operate along this stretch of Waterloo Street, too, and look out for the cage containing turtles and a sleepy old snake: make a donation, touch one of the creatures inside, and it's said that good luck will come your way.

## Sri Krishnan Temple

Waterloo St. The Sri Krishnan Hindu Temple began life in 1870, when it amounted to nothing more than a thatched hut containing a statue of Lord Krishna under a banyan tree. Today it's a popular venue for Hindu weddings, and its unlovely concrete exterior yields a long cast list of gaudily painted Hindu deities.

## Sculpture Square

Now called Sculpture Square, the unassuming, deconsecrated church at the junction of Middle Road and Waterloo Street was erected in the 1870s as the Christian Institute, where residents could debate and read about their faith. After a short stint as the focal point for Singapore's Methodist missionaries, the building became a girls' school in 1894, before transforming into a Church for the Malay community. Today, its grounds and interior gallery space feature contemporary works by local artists, and it has a pleasant café in the courtyard out back, a peaceful place to pause from sightseeing.

▲ KUAN YIM TEMPLE

## Shops

### Jim Thompson Silk Shop

01-07 Raffles Hotel Arcade, 328 North Bridge Rd. The Thai Silk Company was created by American businessman, Jim Thompson, in the middle of the last century. Thompson himself famously and mysteriously disappeared in Malaysia's Cameron Highlands in 1967, but his name lives on in this small concession of his business. Its silk bags, clothes, cushions and cuddly toys are of superior quality – and price.

### Sim Lim Square

1 Rochor Canal Rd. Over 400 electronics, camera, digital and IT software and hardware dealers push their wares in this six-floor mall, ensuring the broadest range of products on the island. Many tourists never get beyond the first couple of floors, meaning prices can be cheaper on the upper levels. It pays to do some research before you come, so you can get a true picture of the discounts on offer.

### Sin Chew Chinese Cultural Products Supermarket

01-00 Skyline Bldg, 192 Waterloo St. Chaotic shop selling images of Chinese Taoist and Buddhist deities, trinkets, necklaces, books and other Buddhist-related goods.

### TeaJoy

01-05 North Bridge Centre, 420 North Bridge Rd. TeaJoy houses a dandy collection of Chinese tea sets – with special attention paid to oolong accoutrements – and glazed porcelain ware.

## Eating

### Fatty's Wing Seong Restaurant

01-31 Burlington Sq, 175 Bencoolen St. Daily noon–11pm. A no-frills Singapore institution where every dish on the long Cantonese menu is cooked to perfection and speedily delivered. A full meal plus beer will cost around $20.

### Imperial Herbal Restaurant

3rd floor, *Metropole Hotel*, 41 Seah St ⓣ63370491. The place to go if you are concerned about your Yin and Yang balance: a resident Chinese physician recommends either cooling or "heaty" dishes. For migraine sufferers, scorpions pickled in some foul-tasting liquor are a must; rheumatics should opt for crispy black ants.

### Rendezvous Restaurant

02-02 *Hotel Rendezvous*, 9 Bras Basah Rd. Daily 11am–9pm. This revered *nasi padang* joint turns out lip-smacking curries, *rendang*s and *sambal*s; the weighing machine in the corner is an unusual touch.

### Tiffin Room

*Raffles Hotel*, 1 Beach Rd ⓣ63371886. Though tiffin lunch (noon–2.30pm) and dinner (7–10.30pm) both cost over $40 per person, the spread of North Indian savouries and sweets and the charming colonial surroundings make them worth considering. Between tiffin sittings, from 3.30pm to 5.30pm, high tea is served ($37).

### Victoria Street Food Court

83 Victoria St. Serving into the wee hours, this open-fronted food court, with around ten stalls, is good for evening seafood and Chinese specialities.

### Yet Con Chicken Rice Restaurant

25 Purvis St ☎63376819. Daily 10.30am–9.30pm. Cheap and cheerful old-time restaurant: try "crunchy, crispy" roast pork with pickled cabbage and radish, or chicken rice, washed down with barley water ($15 for two people).

## Bars

### Balaclava

01-01b Suntec City Convention Centre, 1 Raffles Blvd. Mon–Thurs 3pm–1am, Fri & Sat 3pm–2am. A homage to G-Plan or a nod to 1960s James Bond movies? Both could be said of this retro jazz bar, whose leather chairs, sassy red lamps and dark-wood veneers may make the ambience too oppressive for some tastes. Happy hour is 3pm to 9pm, and there's live jazz nightly from 8.30pm.

### Bar and Billiards Room

*Raffles Hotel*, 1 Beach Rd. Daily 11.30am–midnight. A Singapore Sling in the elegant colonial hotel where the drink was invented is a must on a visit to Singapore. You can also play billiards here (tables are charged by the hour) and snacks are available through the afternoon.

### Liberté

01-19/20 CHIJMES, 30 Victoria St ☎63388481. Mon–Wed 5pm–2am, Thurs–Sat 5pm–3am, Sun 4pm–1am. *Liberté* holds centre stage on CHIJMES' main square – and rightly so. Its artsy wall hangings, flickering tea lights, mellow, Middle Eastern-influenced sounds and excellent cocktails make it one of the few CHIJMES addresses where you actually want to stay inside, rather than head out onto the terrace. Better still, there are free drinks for ladies from 9pm to midnight on Thursdays.

### Long Bar

Raffles Hotel, 1 Beach Rd. The days of British colonial rule is the theme in this tourist-focussed bar, where fans whirr overhead, and Singapore Slings and cold beer are the order of the day. Upstairs there's live music every night.

▲ BAR AND BILLIARDS ROOM *RAFFLES* HOTEL

▲ *LIBERTÉ*, CHIJMES

**Lot, Stock and Barrel Pub**

29 Seah St. Daily 4pm–midnight. Unpretentious boozer, frequented early by office crowds and later by backpackers (the guesthouses of Beach and North Bridge roads are just around the corner), who come for the rock classics on the jukebox. Happy hour is from 4pm to 8pm.

**Paulaner Bräuhaus**

01-01 Millennia Walk, 9 Raffles Blvd ☎68832572. Mon–Thurs & Sun 11.30am–1am, Fri & Sat 11.30am–2am. Lager is very much the drink of choice amidst the copper brewing vats in the downstairs bar of this German-themed restaurant-cum-microbrewery that gets predictably busy around Oktoberfest-time. The restaurant upstairs serves generous platters of *wurst*, *kartoffeln* and *sauerkraut*.

▲ PAULANER BRÄUHAUS

# Fort Canning Park and the western quays

**Hilltop Fort Canning Park is spacious and breezy, and offers respite from, as well as fine views of, Singapore's crowded streets. Tiered and semi-wooded, there are several open spaces where you could comfortably while away an hour or two. The park houses two theatres, cannons, the colonial flagstaff and a lighthouse, as well as the Battle Box, a warren of tunnels that brings Singapore's World War II history to life. Around the foot of the hill, a cluster of tourist attractions sheds further light on Singaporean history and culture, most notably the National Museum, newly reopened after a top-to-toe restoration project. From the southern skirts of Fort Canning Hill, the Singapore River threads west further into the island, passing the godowns (warehouses) of Clarke Quay and Robertson Quay – once hotbeds of colonial commerce and now hotspots in Singapore's clubbing scene. A towpath along the north bank allows for a pleasing twenty-minute walk to Robertson Quay, or there is the more relaxed option of a river taxi.**

▲ THE *KERAMAT*, FORT CANNING PARK

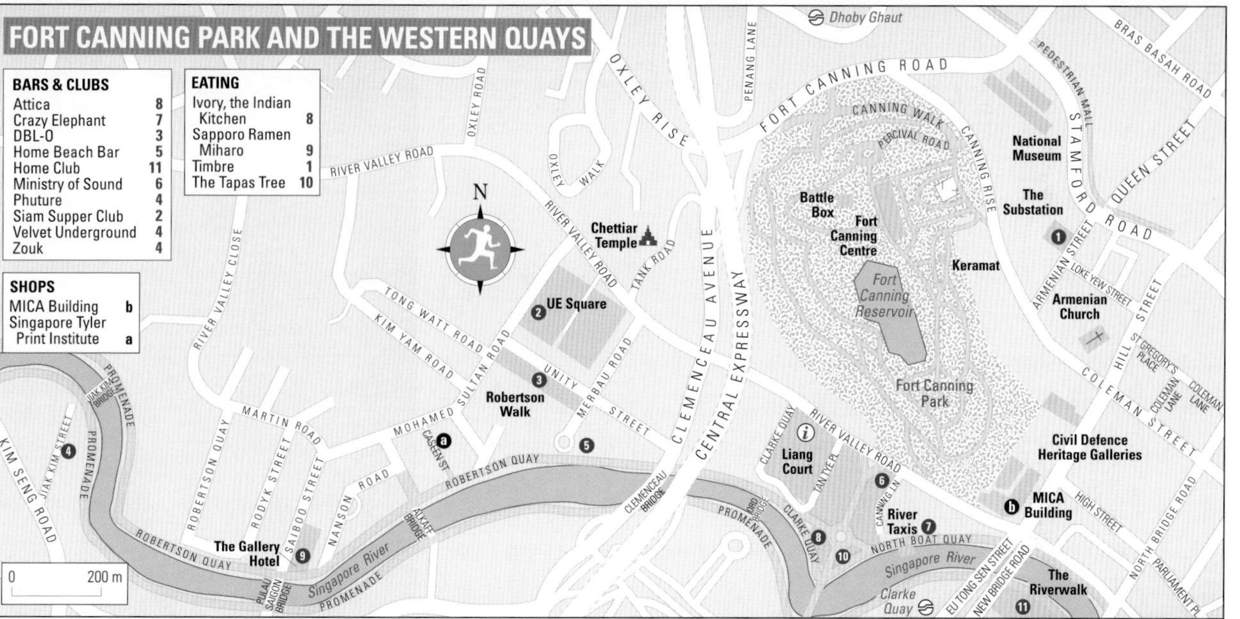
FORT CANNING PARK AND THE WESTERN QUAYS
BARS & CLUBS
Attica 8
Crazy Elephant 7
DBL-O 3
Home Beach Bar 5
Home Club 11
Ministry of Sound 6
Phuture 4
Siam Supper Club 2
Velvet Underground 4
Zouk 4
EATING
Ivory, the Indian Kitchen 8
Sapporo Ramen Miharo 9
Timbre 1
The Tapas Tree 10
SHOPS
MICA Building b
Singapore Tyler Print Institute a
Dhoby Ghaut
Fort Canning Road
Penang Lane
Oxley Rise
Oxley Road
Oxley Walk
River Valley Road
River Valley Close
Tong Watt Road
Kim Yam Road
Sultan Road
Unity Street
Merbau Road
Tank Road
Chettiar Temple
UE Square
Robertson Walk
Mohamed Sultan Road
Caseen St
Martin Road
Robertson Quay
Rodyk Street
Saiboo Street
Nanson Road
The Gallery Hotel
Alkaff Bridge
Pulau Saigon Bridge
Singapore River
Promenade
Jiak Kim Bridge
Jiak Kim Street
Kim Seng Road
Clemenceau Avenue
Clemenceau Bridge
Central Expressway
Canning Walk
Percival Road
Canning Rise
Battle Box
Fort Canning Centre
Fort Canning Reservoir
Keramat
Fort Canning Park
Clarke Quay
Liang Court
Tan Tye Pl
Canning Ln
River Taxis
North Boat Quay
Ord Bridge
National Museum
The Substation
Stamford Road
Pedestrian Mall
Bras Basah Road
Queen Street
Armenian Street
Loke Yew Street
Armenian Church
Hill Street
St Gregory's Place
Coleman Lane
Coleman Street
Civil Defence Heritage Galleries
MICA Building
High Street
North Bridge Road
Parliament Pl
Eu Tong Sen Street
New Bridge Road
The Riverwalk
0
200 m

## Fort Canning Park

When Raffles first caught sight of Singapore, the hill that is now Fort Canning Park was known locally as Bukit Larangan (Forbidden Hill): one of the five ancient Malay kings of Singapura, Sultan Iskandar Shah, reputedly lies here, and a *keramat*, or auspicious place, on the eastern slope of the hill marks the supposed site of his grave. Though only an unassuming lean-to, the *keramat* still attracts a trickle of Muslim pilgrims, as well as childless couples who offer prayers here for fertility. When the British arrived in Singapore, they displayed typical colonial tact by promptly having the hill cleared of its forestation and building a residence on the summit for the governor. This was replaced in 1859 by a fort, though only its gateway, guardhouse and an adjoining wall remain. An early European cemetery survives, however, upon whose stones are engraved intriguing epitaphs to nineteenth-century sailors, traders and residents – among them the pioneering colonial architect, George Coleman. If you circumnavigate the park on its network of paths, look out for some truly magnificent old trees on the western side.

## The Battle Box

Tues–Sun 10am–6pm. Adults $8.

On the northwest flank of Fort Canning Hill lies the Battle Box, the underground operations complex from which the Allied war effort in Singapore was masterminded. The complex uses audio and video effects and animatronics to bring to life the events leading up to the decision by British officers to surrender Singapore to Japanese occupation on February 15, 1942. Authentic, if a little clunky, it provides an engaging enough context to Singapore's darkest hour. Conceived as a gas- and bomb-proof operations chamber, the Battle Box was completed in October 1939, after which it became a part of the Malaya Command World War II Headquarters. Following faithful restoration of its 26 rooms, the complex now conveys a palpable sense of the claustrophobia and tension suffered by the British as the Japanese bore down

▲ THE BATTLE BOX

▲ THE ARMENIAN CHURCH

upon Singapore. The tour of the chambers takes you from the signals room to the cipher chamber (where the air crackles with the rat-tat-tat of Morse sets and the furious tapping of typewriters and coding machines), and from there to a theatrical climax in the conference room, where life-sized figures act out the debate that convinced Lieutenant-General Arthur Percival, the head of Allied Command for Malaya, that surrender was the only option open to him.

## Armenian Church

Hill St. On the eastern edge of Fort Canning Park, the tiny, pearly white Armenian Church of St Gregory the Illuminator was designed by George Coleman in 1835, making it one of the oldest buildings in Singapore. The bell turret that first topped the church was long ago replaced with a spire, topped with a ball and cross; the church's impressive colonnades and elegant louvred windows, though, are original features. Inside is a single, circular chamber, fronted by a marble altar and a painting of the Last Supper; the pews are backed, unusually, with woven rattan. Back outside, among the white gravestones and statues in the church's frangipani-scented gardens is the tombstone of Agnes Joaquim, a nineteenth-century Armenian resident of Singapore, after whom the national flower, the delicate, purple Vanda Miss Joaquim Orchid, is named; she discovered the orchid in her garden and had it registered at the Botanic Gardens.

## Civil Defence Heritage Galleries

62 Hill St. Tues–Sun 10am–5pm. Free. Housed within the splendid red-and-white-striped Central Fire Station, the Civil Defence Heritage Galleries trace the history of firefighting in Singapore from the formation of the first Voluntary Fire Brigade in 1869. The displays, all beautifully restored and buffed up, include old helmets, extinguishers, hand-drawn escape ladders and steam fire engines, while upstairs there are explanations of current equipment and practices. More

▲ STAINED GLASS DOME AT THE NATIONAL MUSEUM

compelling are the accounts of the island's two most destructive fires: the Bukit Ho Swee fire of 1961, which claimed four lives and 16,000 homes when it ripped through a district of atap-thatched huts and timber yards; and the blaze in Robinson's department store in Raffles Place, in 1972, when a short circuit in old wires led to nine deaths.

The Central Fire Station itself remains operational. When it was first built in 1908, the watchtower was the tallest building in the region, making it easy for firemen to scan the downtown area for fires.

### The Substation

53 Armenian St ⓣ63377800, ⓦwww.substation.org. This disused power station has been converted into a multimedia arts centre, with film showings, theatrical productions, dance, performance art and exhibitions all featuring in its rolling schedule. In the courtyard outside, a flea market takes place every Sunday afternoon, with bric-a-brac stalls selling anything from local crafts to second-hand Russian watches. It's a great place for people-watching, though you might not find much you want to buy.

### National Museum

93 Stamford Rd ⓣ63323251, ⓦnationalmuseum.sg. Daily 10am–6pm. Due to reopen in December 2006 following a top-to-bottom renovation, the National Museum is immediately distinguishable by the eye-catching dome of stained glass that tops its entrance. Central to the revamped museum will be the eleven artefacts deemed to be the treasures of the museum. Amongst these are: fourteenth-century Javanese gold relics found on Fort Canning Hill; a coffin cover from a Straits Chinese funeral; a Fujian glove puppet theatre stage dating from the 1930s; and a fragment of the Singapore Stone, a three-metre high boulder that stood in the mouth of the Singapore River, and whose ancient Sumatran script has never been deciphered. Another main pillar of the collection will be the Singapore History Gallery, which promises to take a "storytelling" approach to the island's history.

The National Museum was originally opened in 1887 as the Raffles Museum and Library, and soon acquired a reputation for the excellence of its natural history collection. In 1969, the place was given its current name in recognition of Singapore's independence, and subsequently altered its bias towards local history and culture. Out front, a stack of silver triangles marks the site of the Singapore Millennium Time Capsule, to be opened in January 2050; near it stands a chunky slate statue of t'ai chi boxers by Taiwanese sculptor, Ju Ming.

### The western quays

South of Fort Canning Park, River Valley Road sweeps west past Clarke Quay, a grid of nineteenth-century godowns (warehouses), renovated into an entertainments complex. The quay is fast becoming a focal point for Singaporean clubbers – a shift underlined by the fact that it now houses the new *Ministry of Sound*. Robertson Quay, further inland from Clarke Quay, has further extended the gentrification of the Singapore River. Restaurants, bars and hotels are cropping up beside its banks in increasing numbers – though one or two pleasingly tumbledown godowns still survive, inland of Pulau Saigon Bridge. Singapore's own most iconic club, *Zouk*, is a stone's throw away, south of the river on Jiak Kim Street.

## Shops

### MICA Building

140 Hill St. Daily 11am–9pm. Home to the Ministry of Information, Communication and the Arts, the MICA Building houses Singapore's greatest concentration of art galleries; the Cape of Good Hope and Gajah galleries both carry a lot of Asian works, while Art-2 focuses in on contemporary Burmese artists in particular.

### Singapore Tyler Print Institute

41 Robertson Quay. Tues–Fri 10am–6pm, Sat 10am–8pm. Housed in a nineteenth-century riverside godown, the state-of-the-art, non-profit STPI works with local artists to print their original works. As well as a print- and paper-making workshop, it's also an art exhibition space-cum-print shop. Workshops are also laid on for kids.

## Eating

### Ivory, the Indian Kitchen

02-04, Block A, Clarke Quay. Indian fine dining in contemporary surroundings: *Ivory*'s extensive menu draws in influences from India's coastal states, with dishes including Goan chicken Xacutti (chicken in spiced coconut sauce) and Karnatakan pan-fried tiger prawns.

### Sapporo Ramen Miharo

*Gallery Hotel*, Robertson Quay. At this small Japanese noodle soup address within the *Gallery Hotel*, you can just sit up at one of the slatted wooden bar stools and choose from the various *ramen* soups pictured.

### The Tapas Tree

01-08, Block D, Clarke Quay. Daily 11.30am–midnight. The paellas, hot and cold tapas dishes and sangria served here bring a touch of the Mediterranean to Clarke Quay's waterfront dining scene. Latino guest bands extend the theme nightly.

### Timbre

45 Armenian St. Mon–Sat 6pm–1am. This charming alfresco dining option, set under the palm trees of the Substation garden, offers a wide-ranging menu that stretches from bangers and mash and pork ribs to kebabs and barbecued fish. The joint is popular with the local student population, who come in numbers for the nightly live bands.

## Bars

### Crazy Elephant

01-07 Trader's Market, Clarke Quay ☎63371990. Mon–Thurs & Sun 5pm–1am, Fri & Sat 5pm–2am. Friendly

*Crazy Elephant* plays rock music on the turntables between live sessions by the house blues band, with happy hour from 5pm to 9pm daily. The decor comprises wood panelling and graffiti, but regulars prefer the tables out by the water's edge.

### Home Beach Bar

15 Merbau Rd ⓣ68352413. Daily 3pm–1am. The deckchairs, lanterns, and reggae sounds at this mellow riverfront venue, where happy hour lasts from 5pm to 8pm, bring a little touch of the Caribbean to Singapore.

### Siam Supper Club

01-53/55 UE Square, 207 River Valley Rd ⓣ67350938. Mon–Sat 3pm–3am. Semicircular red leather booths, a circular bar and lustrous red oval lamps render the *Supper Club* sassily contemporary, while Buddha effigies in wall niches add an Asian twist. Bar snacks range from chicken wings to sashimi, and cocktails are $12, with happy hour from 5pm to 9pm.

## Clubs

### Attica

01-12 Clarke Quay ⓣ63339973, ⓦwww.attica.com.sg. Daily 5pm–3am. Cover charge $25. *Attica* is an ultra-hip nightspot with distinct themed areas – alfresco space with river views and Latino jazz; laid-back lounge area; Balinese-themed courtyard; and heaving dance floor – meaning that you'll find a spot to please you, whatever your mood. The cocktails are well mixed.

### DBL-O

01-24 Robertson Walk, 11 Unity St ⓣ67352008, ⓦwww.dbl-o.com. Wed–Sat 8pm–3am. Cover charge $15–25, depending on the night; Wed night is free for women. With its massive dance floor and three separate bar areas, roomy *DBL-O* really can pack in the punters. House, garage and R&B are the favoured musical styles.

▲ CRAZY ELEPHANT

▲ MINISTRY OF SOUND

**Home Club**

B01-06 The Riverwalk, 20 Upper Circular Road Ⓦwww.homeclub.com.sg. Daily except Mon 9pm–3am. Cover charge around $20 most nights. The fringes of a shopping mall might seem a strange place for a happening club, but this cosy venue makes the best of its riverside location with a chilled-out patio area outside; inside DJs spin a range of sounds, from R&B to Eighties synth-pop depending on the evening. Friday nights see a switch to indie, however, as a bunch of local bands play original material that wouldn't sound out of place on US college radio.

**Ministry of Sound**

The Cannery, River Valley Rd Ⓦwww.ministryofsound.com.sg. Wed–Sun 9pm–4am. Cover charge of around $20 most nights, though women get in free on Wed. Claiming to be the largest *MoS* franchise in the world, and spilling over into various annexes, this heavyweight club boasts regular appearances by big-name DJs, a water feature doubling as a screen for visuals, and sounds ranging from funky house to R&B and soul.

**Phuture**

17 Jiak Kim St Ⓣ67382988, Ⓦwww.zoukclub.com.sg. Tues–Sat 9pm–3am. Cover charge $18 for women, $25 for men. Housed in the same venue as *Zouk*, *Phuture* is a dark, smoky joint, with harder hip-hop, break beat and drum and bass sounds than *Zouk* and therefore a more youthful crowd.

**Velvet Underground**

17 Jiak Kim St Ⓣ67382988, Ⓦwww.zoukclub.com.sg. Tues–Sat 9pm–3am. Cover charge $25 for women, $35 for men; includes access to *Zouk* and *Phuture*. Less thumping than *Phuture* and *Zouk*, *Velvet Underground* has a dreamy and chilled ambience, enhanced by the use of lava lamps.

**Zouk**

17 Jiak Kim St Ⓣ67382988, Ⓦwww.zoukclub.com.sg. Wed–Sat 7pm–3am. Cover charge $15 before 9pm, then $25. The first of Singapore's truly cool club venues uses palm trees and Moorish tiles to create a Mediterranean feel. Famous DJs, such as Paul Oakenfold, guest regularly.

# Orchard Road and around

**Orchard Road is synonymous with shopping. Huge and ever-more futuristic malls crowd the street, and pavements are thick with tourists and domestic shoppers seeking out bargains. The area is barely less busy at night, when its many restaurants, bars and clubs come into their own. Happily, the bustle and traffic of the road is counterbalanced by the two open spaces that book-end it – the colourful and well-groomed Singapore Botanic Gardens to the west, and the grounds of the Istana, the President's residence, to the east. In the few remaining Peranakan houses on Emerald Hill, there is also a welcome reminder of a time when this district was home only to nutmeg plantations and the occasional monied family home. Orchard Road is served by three MRT stations: Dhoby Ghaut, Somerset and Orchard. Alighting at Orchard will leave you bang in the centre of the classiest and most varied stretch of shopping malls.**

## Istana Negara Singapura

Ⓦ www.istana.gov.sg. Grounds open public hols only 8.30am–6pm (check website for details). $1 for foreigners; free for locals. You'll have to be in Singapore on a public holiday

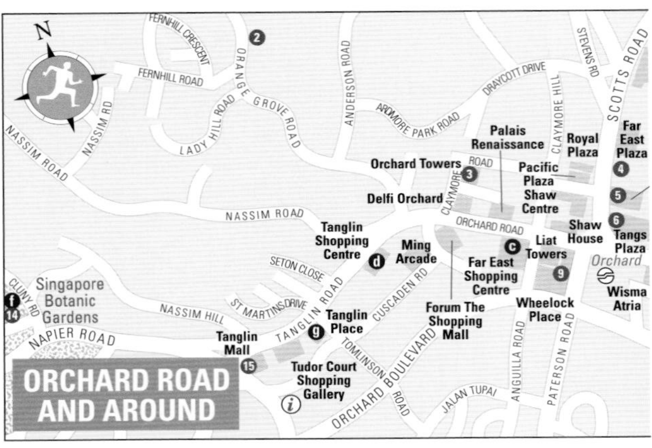


**EATING**

| | |
|---|---|
| Blu | 2 |
| Crystal Jade La Mian Xiao Long Bao | 5 & 13 |
| Don Noodle Bistro | 15 |
| Food Republic | 10 |
| Halia | 14 |
| Newton Circus Hawker Centre | 1 |
| Nooch | 9 |
| Sakae Sushi | 9 |
| Top of the M | 12 |

**BARS & CLUBS**

| | |
|---|---|
| Alley Bar | 11 |
| Bar None | 6 |
| Brix | 4 |
| Harry's @ Orchard | 3 |

▲ GUARD AT THE ISTANA GATE

to get beyond the stern-looking soldiers that guard the gate of the Istana Negara Singapura. Built in 1869, the istana, with its ornate cornices, elegant louvred shutters, verandahs and high mansard roof, was originally the official residence of Singapore's British governors. On independence it became the residence of the president of Singapore – currently S.R. Nathan – whose portrait you'll see in banks, post offices and shops across the state. During public holiday open days the president goes walkabout around the istana grounds as thousands of Singaporeans flock to picnic on the well-landscaped lawns, local brass bands belt out jaunty tunes, and martial arts teams provide demonstrations. If you're in Singapore on the first Sunday of the month, it's worth dropping by the istana at 5.45pm to witness the changing of the guard ceremony at the gates.

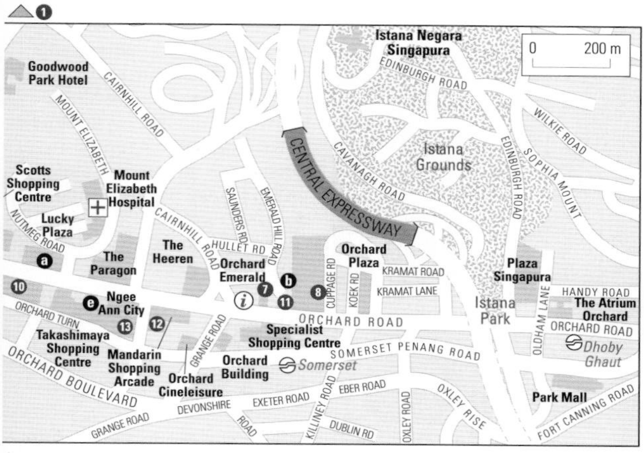


No. 5 Emerald Hill 7
Xpose Café 8

**SHOPS**

Amir & Sons a
Antiques of the Orient d
Books Kinokuniya e
Kwok Gallery c
Lopburi g
One Price Store b
Richard Hung Jewellers a
Risis f
Select Books d
Shanghai Tang e

### Emerald Hill Road

On Emerald Hill Road, which runs north from Somerset MRT station, a clutch of architecturally notable houses have survived Singapore's wrecking ball. Emerald Hill was granted to Englishman William Cuppage in 1845 and for some years afterwards was the site of a large nutmeg plantation. After Cuppage's death in 1872, the land was sold off, much of it to members of the Peranakan community that had evolved in Malaya as a result of the intermarriage between early Chinese settlers and Malay women. A walk up Emerald Hill Road takes you past exquisitely crafted houses dating from this period, built in a decorative architectural style known as Chinese Baroque, which is typified by highly coloured ceramic tiles, carved swing doors, shuttered windows and pastel-shaded walls with fine plaster mouldings.

Back towards Orchard Road on Cuppage Terrace, halfway along Cuppage Road on the left, is an unusually (for Orchard Road) old row of shophouses, where a burgeoning restaurant and bar scene has developed.

▲ PERANAKAN HOUSE, EMERALD HILL ROAD

### Singapore Botanic Gardens

Cluny Rd. Botanic Gardens open daily 5am–midnight; free. National Orchid Garden open daily 8.30am–7pm; $5. Just a ten-minute walk beyond the western end of Orchard Road, the open space of Singapore Botanic Gardens provides some welcome respite after a few hours' shopping. The gardens were founded in 1859 when the Agri-Horticultural Society was granted 32 hectares of land by the government to create a public park, and it was here, in 1877, that the Brazilian seeds from which grew the great rubber plantations of Malaysia were first nurtured. The fifty-odd hectares of land feature a mini-jungle, rose garden, topiary, fernery, palm valley and lakes that are home to turtles and swans. There's also the National Orchid Garden, which boasts over a thousand species. At dawn and dusk, joggers and students of t'ai chi haunt the lawns and paths of the gardens, while at the weekend, newlyweds bundle down from church for their photos to be taken. You can pick up a free map of the grounds at the ranger's office, a little to the right of the main gate, on Cluny Road.

## Shops

### Amir & Sons

03-01/7 Lucky Plaza, 304 Orchard Rd. Having traded since 1921, Amir & Sons is said to be the oldest carpet-seller in Singapore, and stocks fine carpets from Persia, Pakistan, Turkey and China.

▲ SINGAPORE BOTANIC GARDENS

**Antiques of the Orient**

02-40 Tanglin Shopping Centre, 19 Tanglin Rd. Specialists in antiquarian Asian books, maps and prints. Whether you want a first edition of a Bornean travel account, or a framed copy of a botanical sketch of a rainforest fruit, this is the place to visit.

**Books Kinokuniya**

03-10/15 Ngee Ann City, 391 Orchard Rd. Singapore's largest bookstore by a long way, with an excellent selection of novels, magazines and travel guidebooks. Asian authors and books of local interest merit their own section.

**Kwok Gallery**

03-01 Far East Shopping Centre, 545 Orchard Rd. The Kwoks have been amassing and selling antique Chinese art works for nearing a century, and their inventory of porcelainware and paintings is accordingly broad and impressive.

**Lopburi**

01-04 Tanglin Place, 91 Tanglin Rd. A treasure-trove of a store, selling seriously fine – and seriously expensive – antique Buddhas and Khmer sculptures, as well as some old silk textiles.

**One Price Store**

3 Emerald Hill Rd. This venerable old shop, fronted by a jungle of potted plants, carries everything from carved camphorwood chests to Chinese snuff bottles. Sadly, not everything is one price.

**Richard Hung Jewellers**

01-24 Lucky Plaza, 304 Orchard Rd. All the staff are qualified

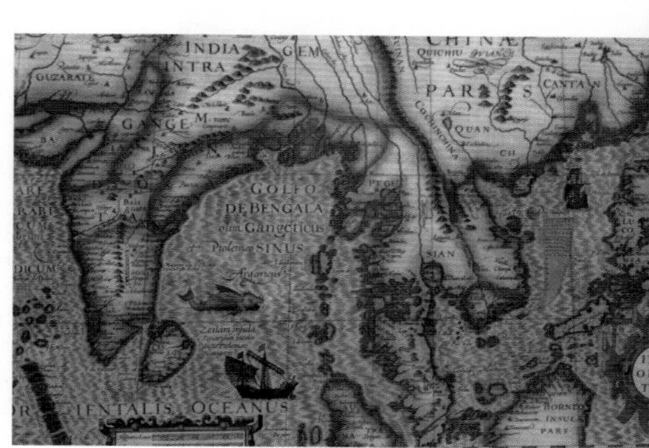


▲ ANTIQUES OF THE ORIENT

gemologists at this well-regarded jewellers, which has specialized in gems and pearls for a quarter of a century.

### Risis

Singapore Botanic Gardens, Cluny Rd. Risis specializes in jewellery made by silver and gold-plating flora of all sorts – from ferns to orchids. Pieces start at around $35.

### Select Books

03-15 Tanglin Shopping Centre, 19 Tanglin Rd. This modestly-sized store crams in a huge array of specialist books on Southeast Asian culture, history, politics and wildlife. If you want to get under the skin of this region, there's no better place to start.

### Shanghai Tang

02-09 Ngee Ann City, 391 Orchard Rd. Exotic silk tunics and other high-fashion, Hong Kong-designed Chinoiserie are available at Shanghai Tang. As well as clothes for men, women and children, look out for eye-catching picture frames, candles, stationery and other homeware.

▲ SHOPPERS ON ORCHARD ROAD

## Eating

### Blu

*Shangri-La Hotel*, Orange Grove Rd ☎67302598. One of Singapore's most exquisite dining experiences: California fusion cuisine of the highest quality, overlooking downtown Singapore from *Shangri-La*'s 24th floor. Mains might include roasted Alaskan halibut with vegetable tempura ($45) or duo of Japanese *wagyu* beef ($85).

### Crystal Jade La Mian Xiao Long Bao

Ngee Ann City 04-27 ☎62381661; Scotts Shopping Centre #B1-05 ☎67340200. Very popular chain specializing in Shanghai and Beijing cuisine. The name is a bit of a mouthful, but encapsulates their signature dishes – *xiao long bao*, incredibly succulent pork dumplings, and *la mian*, literally "pulled noodles", in which the strands of dough are stretched and worked by hand (the version cooked with wood-ear fungus is particularly good). It's not great for vegetarians, though veggie versions of a few dishes can be made to order.

### Don Noodle Bistro

01-16 Tanglin Mall, 163 Tanglin Rd ☎67383188. Daily 11.30am–10.30pm. Minimalist yet chic, *Don* is something of a paradox – a Western-style take on the noodle bar, imported back to the East. The menu is not country-specific, meaning that you can enjoy Indonesian *kway teow goreng* (fried flat noodles) while your dining companion tucks into Japanese *ramen* noodles.

**Food Republic**

4th floor, Wisma Atria, 435 Orchard Rd. Smashing a/c food court offering *kaya* toast and strong coffee for breakfast, then tandoori, noodles, Japanese specialities and a host of other menu options for lunch and dinner.

**Halia**

Singapore Botanic Gardens, 1 Cluny Rd ⓣ64766711. Daily 11am–11pm, plus Sat & Sun 8–10.30am for breakfast. Moonlit and candlelit after dusk, *Halia*'s magical garden-verandah setting whisks you a world away from downtown Singapore. The East-meets-West lunch menu spans sandwiches, pasta and laksa; at night, there are more substantial but still moderately priced dishes such as rack of lamb and seafood stew. The high-tea deal (daily 3–5.30pm) offers cake and coffee or tea – or take along the papers and tuck into the weekend buffet breakfast.

**Newton Circus Hawker Centre**

North end of Scotts Road; MRT to Newton. Firmly on the mainstream tourist trail, prices are a little higher at Newton Circus than at other hawker centres, but it has the advantage of staying open until late (as long as there are customers). It's particularly noted for its seafood stalls, and is looking far smarter, after a recent refurb.

▲ NEWTON CIRCUS HAWKER CENTRE

**Nooch**

02-16 Wheelock Place, 501 Orchard Rd ⓣ62350880. Mon–Fri noon–3pm & 6–10.30pm, Sat & Sun noon–11pm. The blurb on its menu calls this cool and popular, moderately priced, crescent-shaped joint overlooking Orchard Boulevard a "nondestinational" restaurant – meaning that the idea is to order and scoff down your MSG-free Thai or Japanese noodles on the double, and be on your way. The Thai *tub tim krob*, or water chestnuts in coconut milk, is a good way to douse the fires after a *tom yam kung* soup.

**Sakae Sushi**

02-13 Wheelock Place, 501 Orchard Rd ⓣ67376281. Daily noon–10pm. Part of a popular chain, this sushi and sashimi bar, bang in the centre of Orchard Road, has sushi set lunches that start from $12. Diners can choose either to sit up at the conveyor-belt bar, or at diner-style booths.

**Top of the M**

*Meritus Mandarin Hotel*, 333 Orchard Rd ⓣ68316258. Revolving 170m above Orchard Road, *Top of the M* gives you the chance to scan all points north, east, south and west of downtown Singapore while you dine on the French-influenced cuisine. The champagne brunch (Sun noon–

3pm) offers free flow of bubbly, plus snacks, for $45 a head.

# Bars

### Alley Bar

2 Emerald Hill Rd ☎67388818. Sun–Thurs 5pm–2am, Fri & Sat 5pm–3am. Part alley and part shophouse, the *Alley Bar* uses potted ferns, old mirrors and Peranakan antiques to rekindle the spirit of back-street Singapore half a century ago. The candlelit, setteed area behind the bar is cosiest.

### Harry's @ Orchard

01-05 Orchard Towers, 1 Claymore Drive ☎67367330. Mon–Fri 3pm–2am, Sat 11am–3am, Sun 11am–1am. Tania, the legendary local covers band, belt out Beatles, Santana and Eagles classics to an adoring crowd every night. At the bar, there's a broad range of beers, cocktails and shooters to choose from and *Harry's* has a decent tapas menu too. Happy hour lasts until 9pm daily.

### No.5 Emerald Hill

5 Emerald Hill Rd ☎67320818. Daily noon–2am. Housed in a charming, 1910-built Peranakan-style shophouse, *No. 5* emphasizes its antiquity by its use of Persian carpets and period-detail Chinese teak and rosewood carvings. The lychee martinis are first class and the bar menu, spanning pizzas, chicken wings and other snacks, isn't bad either. Happy hour is from noon to 9pm and 1am to 2am.

### Xpose Café

49 Cuppage Terrace. Daily 4pm–midnight. Gay bar just off Orchard Road, serving decent Thai food, but best avoided on Wednesday, Friday and Saturday unless you are prepared to take the karaoke mike.

▲ BAR AT *NO. 5 EMERALD HILL*

# Clubs

### Bar None

*Marriott Hotel*, 320 Orchard Rd. Daily 7pm–3am. Cover charge Fri & Sat $20 for women, $25 for men. With its retro modular furniture, stone walls, pop art and sleek wooden floors, *Bar None* is as eclectic as it is popular. The mezzanine area is more relaxed than the rocking dance floor below, where house band Jive Talkin' belt out current hits nightly.

### Brix

*Grand Hyatt Hotel*, 10–12 Scotts Rd. Daily 7pm–2am. Cover charge $20. Despite its roughed-up decor (bare brick walls and wood panels), basement club *Brix* attracts a glamorous and monied crowd. On Monday nights, the acid jazz, R&B and hip hop give way to free salsa lessons.

# Chinatown

**Until late into the twentieth century, the two square kilometres of Chinatown were the epicentre of Chinese life and culture in Singapore. Today, the area lies robbed of much of its cultural heritage, scarred by demolition and dwarfed by the skyscrapers of the Central Business District. Even so, amongst its shopping centres and modern housing blocks, a wander through Chinatown's remaining streets unearths musty and atmospheric temples, traditional craft shops, old-style coffee shops and restaurants, and surviving clan association houses – to which early Chinese settlers would turn for assistance with finding food, lodging and work. Provision stores crammed with birds' nests, dried cuttlefish, ginger, chillies, mushrooms and salted fish do a brisk trade, and you might hear the rattle of a game of mah jong being played. As you might expect, Chinatown is a great place to sample high quality Chinese food, though its burgeoning restaurant scene also presents Indian, Peranakan and Western options.**

## Thian Hock Keng Temple

Telok Ayer St. Enormous Thian Hock Keng Temple ("Temple of Heavenly Happiness") is a hugely impressive Hokkien building, and sprucer than ever after a recent makeover. It stands on Telok Ayer Street, whose Malay name ("Watery Bay") recalls a time, before land reclamation, when the street would have run along the shoreline of the Straits of Singapore. The temple was built on the site of a small joss house where immigrants stepping ashore made offerings to Ma Chu Por (or Tian Hou), the queen of heaven, to thank her for their safe passage – a statue of the goddess, dating to 1842, stands in the centre of the main hall, flanked by the god of war on the right and the protector of life on the left. The temple looks particularly spectacular from the street: dragons stalk its broad roofs, while the entrance

▲ TEMPLE GUARDIANS AT THIAN HOCK KENG TEMPLE

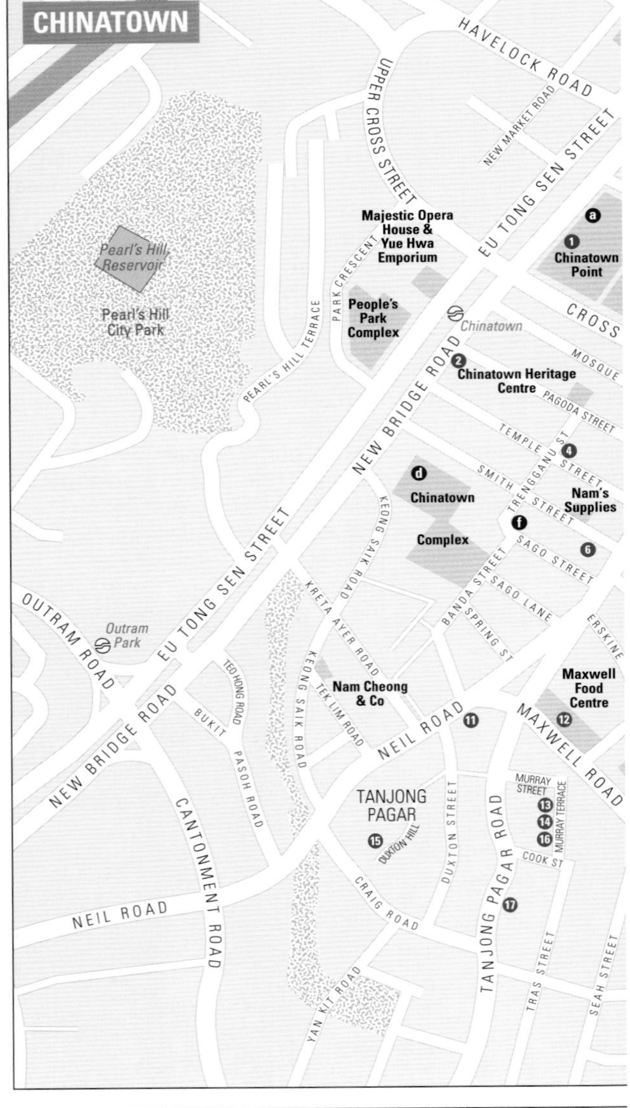


**EATING**

| | | | | | |
|---|---|---|---|---|---|
| Ann Siang 5 | 8 | Chinese Opera Teahouse | 6 | Moti Mahal Restaurant | 13 |
| Bak kwa stalls | 2 | Indochine | 7 | Mouth Restaurant | 1 |
| Blue Ginger | 17 | Lau Pa Sat Festival Market | 10 | Swee Kee | 9 |
| Broth | 15 | Maxwell Food Centre | 12 | Tea Chapter | 11 |
| China Square Food Centre | 5 | Mitzi's | 16 | Ya Kun Kaya Toast | 3 |
| | | Moi Kong Hakka Restaurant | 14 | | |

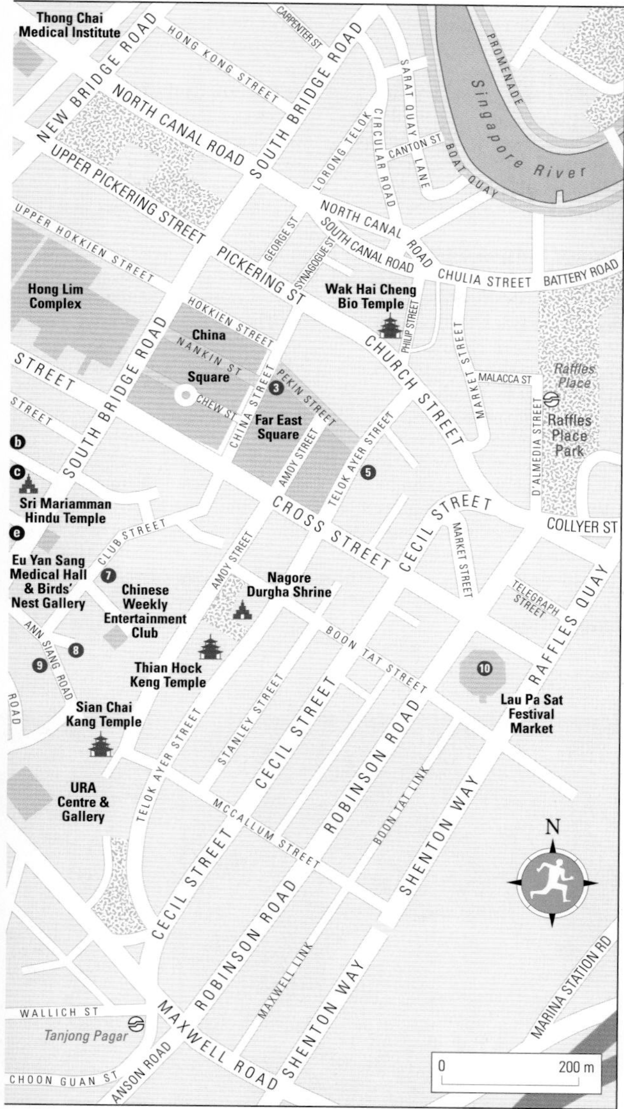


**BARS & CLUBS**

Backstage Bar 4
Bar Savanh 7

**SHOPS & MARKETS**

Chinatown Complex d
Chu's Jade Centre a
Far East Inspirations c
House of Zhen e
Red Peach Gallery b
Singapore Handicraft Centre a
Zhen Lacquer Gallery f

to the temple compound bristles with ceramic flowers, foliage and figures. Two stone lions stand guard at the entrance, and door gods, painted on the front doors, prevent evil spirits from entering. Look out for the huge ovens, always lit, in which offerings to gods and ancestors are burnt.

### Nagore Durgha Shrine

Telok Ayer St. It's a testament to Singapore's multicultural nature that Thian Hock Keng's next-door neighbour should be the Nagore Durgha Shrine, built in the 1820s by Chulias from southern India and dedicated to the ascetic, Shahul Hamid of Nagore. The shrine's tiered minarets, onion domes and Islamic facades have long been in a state of disrepair, but ongoing renovation works are rectifying this slowly.

### Amoy Street

Amoy Street, together with Telok Ayer Street and China Street, to the north, was designated by Singapore's early British rulers as a Hokkien enclave. It's flanked by long terraces of shophouses, all featuring characteristic "five-foot ways", or covered verandahs, which are so called simply because they jut five feet out from the house. A few of the shophouses are in a ramshackle state, but most have been marvellously renovated and bought up by companies in need of some fancy office space.

It's worth walking down to mustard-coloured Sian Chai Kang Temple, at 66 Amoy St. Below the fiery dragons on its roof, it's a musty, open-fronted place dominated by huge urns, full to the brim with ash from untold numbers of burned incense sticks. Guarding the temple are two carved stone lions whose fancy red neck ribbons are said to attract good fortune and prosperity.

▲ WORSHIPPERS AT WAK HAI CHENG BIO TEMPLE

## Wak Hai Cheng Bio Temple

Philip St. An ugly concrete courtyard, crisscrossed by a web of ropes supporting numerous spiralled incense sticks, fronts the Wak Hai Cheg Bio Temple. The temple's name means "Temple of the Calm Sea" – a logical choice for early worshippers who had arrived safely in Singapore – and an effigy of Tian Hou, the queen of heaven and protector of seafarers, is housed in its right-hand chamber. The temple has an incredibly ornate roof, crammed with tiny models of Chinese village scenes; the temple cat meanders across here sometimes, dwarfing the tableaux like a creature from a Godzilla movie.

## Hong Lim Complex

To get a flavour of the old ways that survived before Far East Square subsumed China Street and its offshoots at the turn of the millennium, head to the Hong Lim Complex. It's a modern housing estate, where old men in white T-shirts and striped pyjama trousers sit chewing the cud in walkways lined with medical halls, chop makers, and stores selling birds' nests, pork floss (think savoury candy floss), dried mushrooms and gold jewellery.

## Club Street

At the southern end of China Street, steep Club Street was once noted for its temple-carving shops, though these too have now fallen to the demolition ball and been replaced by swish apartment blocks and swanky bars and restaurants. An impromptu flea market still takes place on the far side of the car park opposite, where traders squat on their haunches surrounded by catalogues, old coins, sleeveless records and phone cards. Sadly even the clan associations and guilds that gave Club Street its name are fast disappearing, though there are still a few to be seen, higher up the hill. These are easy to recognize: black-and-white photos of old members cover the walls, while from upstairs comes the clacking sound of mah jong tiles; behind the screens that almost invariably span the doorway, old men sit and chat. The most notable of the associations is the Chinese Weekly Entertainment Club, at no76 – flanked by roaring lion heads, it's an imposing, 1891-built mansion that was established by a Peranakan millionaire, though not one that non-members can enter.

## Eu Yan Sang Medical Hall

267–271 South Bridge Rd. Mon–Sat 8.30am–6pm. The beautifully renovated Eu Yan Sang Medical Hall offers a great introduction to traditional Chinese medicines: the shop smells a little like a compost heap on a hot day and there is a weird assortment of ingredients on the shelves, which to the uninitiated look more likely to kill than cure. Besides the usual herbs and roots favoured by the Chinese are various dubious remedies derived from exotic and endangered species: blood circulation problems and external injuries are eased with centipedes and insects crushed into a "rubbing liquor"; the ground-up gall bladders of snakes or bears apparently work wonders on pimples; monkeys' gallstones aid asthmatics; and deer penis is supposed to provide a lift to any sexual problem. Antlers, sea horses, scorpions and turtle shells also feature regularly in Chinese prescriptions, though the greatest cure-all of Oriental medicine is said to be ginseng, a

▲ PREPARING A TRADITIONAL REMEDY, EU YAN SANG MEDICAL HALL

clever little root that will combat anything from weakness of the heart to acne and jet lag. If you need a pick-me-up, or are just curious, the shop administers free cups of ginseng tea.

### Birds' Nest Gallery

Eu Yan Sang Medical Hall, 267–271 South Bridge Rd. Mon–Sat 10am–5.30pm. $5. Above the Eu Yan Sang Medical Hall is the small but engaging Birds' Nest Gallery, which casts light on the history, harvesting and processing of this most famous of Chinese delicacies. Birds' nests emerged as a prized supplement among China's royal and noble classes during the Ming Dynasty, and can still command prices to their weight in gold. They are valued for their high glycoprotein, calcium, iron and vitamin B1 content, and for their efficacy in boosting the immune system and curing bronchial ailments. Produced by swiftlets in the limestone and coastal caves of Southeast Asia, birds' nests are a mixture of saliva, moss and grass. It's the painstaking process of picking out this moss and grass by hand that makes the product so expensive – that, and the slow and precarious business of initial harvesting. A screen presentation in English shows nest harvesters or "spidermen" scaling bamboo poles as long as 25 metres in the caves of Borneo, with only the torches attached to the poles to guide them. To visit the gallery, ask a member of staff in Eu Yan Sang.

### Sri Mariamman Hindu Temple

South Bridge Rd. Opposite the Eu Yan Sang Medical Hall, the compound of the Sri Mariamman Hindu Temple bursts with primary-coloured, wild-looking statues of deities and animals. There's always some ritual or other being attended to by one of the temple's priests, drafted in from the subcontinent and dressed in simple loincloths. Once beyond the superb *gopuram* over the front entrance and inside the temple, look up at the roof and you'll see splendidly vivid friezes depicting a host of Hindu deities, including the three manifestations of the supreme being: Brahma the Creator (with three of his four heads showing), Vishnu the Preserver, and Shiva the Destroyer (holding one of his sons). The main sanctum, facing you as you walk inside, is devoted to Goddess Mariamman, who's worshipped for her power to cure disease, while smaller sanctums dotted about the open walkway that runs round the temple honour a host of other deities. In one, a sculpture of the Goddess Periachi Amman portrays her with a queen lying on her lap, whose evil child she has ripped from her womb – odd, then, that she should be the protector of children, to whom one-month-old babies are brought. Sri Aravan, with his bushy moustache and big ears, is far less intimidating; his sanctum is at the back on the right-hand side of the complex.

To the left of the main sanctum there's a patch of sand which, once a year during the festival of Thimithi, is covered in red-hot coals, across which male Hindus run to prove the strength of their faith. The participants, who line up all the way along South Bridge Road waiting their turn, are supposedly protected from the heat of the coals by the power of prayer, though the ambulance parked round the back of the temple suggests that some aren't praying quite hard enough.

## The URA Gallery

URA Centre, 45 Maxwell Rd ⓦwww.ura.gov.sg. Mon–Fri 9am–4.30pm, Sat 9am–12.30pm. Free. A skip around the URA Gallery offers a fascinating insight into the grand designs of Singapore's Urban Redevelopment Authority. Singapore's land architects continue to remould their island like a ball of putty, erasing roads here and reclaiming land there, and at the URA Gallery you can view their blueprint for the island's future. Interactive exhibits, touch-screen terminals and scale models trace Singapore's progress from sleepy backwater to modern metropolis and chart ongoing efforts to reshape and redefine specific regions of the island. But the gallery's emphasis is more upon the future than the past: there's a vast model of the downtown area of Singapore highlighting districts currently under development (which also offers new arrivals to the island the chance to get their bearings) – it's best scrutinized through one of the telescopes set up on the floor above – while elsewhere on the upper floor, you get the chance to control a sky cam high above the city, try your hand at a little municipal planning and learn more about Singapore's state-of-the-art MRT system.

▲ HINDU DEITY, SRI MARIAMMAN TEMPLE

## Tanjong Pagar

The Tanjong Pagar district of Chinatown has changed beyond recognition in the past two decades. Once a veritable sewer of brothels and opium dens, it now has conservation area status, and its two hundred-plus shophouses have been painstakingly restored, painted in pastel hues and converted into bars, restaurants and shops. While touring Tanjong Pagar, it's worth making time for a stop at one of the traditional teahouses along Neil Road, such as *Tea Chapter*.

## Sago Street to Mosque Street

The knot of streets west of South Bridge Road between Sago Street and Mosque Street is tour-bus Chinatown, heaving with gangs of holidaymakers plundering souvenir shops. As recently as the 1950s, Sago Street was home to several "death houses" – rudimentary hospices where skeletal citizens saw out their final hours on rattan camp beds. These houses have all gone, to be replaced by restaurants, bakeries, medicine halls and shops stacked to the rafters with Chinese vases, teapots and jade. Sago, Smith, Temple and Pagoda streets only really recapture their youth around the time of Chinese New Year, when they're crammed to bursting with stalls selling festive branches of blossom, oranges, sausages and waxed chickens – which look as if they have melted to reveal a handful of bones inside. Sago Street skirts to the right of the Chinatown Complex, where its name changes to Trengganu Street. Despite the hordes of tourists, and the shops selling them tat, there are occasional glimpses of Chinatown's old trades and industries, such as Nam's Supplies at 22 Smith St, which offers shirts, Rolex watches, Nokia mobile phones, money, laptops and passports – all made out of paper; the Chinese burn them to ensure that their ancestors don't want for creature comforts in the next life. They even have "Otherworld Bank" credit cards, "Hell Airlines" air tickets and "Hell City" cigarettes. Between the Chinatown Complex and New Bridge Road, Nam Cheong and Co, off nearby Kreta Ayer Road at 01-04 Block, 334 Keong Saik Rd, takes this industry to its logical conclusion, producing huge paper houses and near life-

▲ PAPER CAR, NAM CHEONG AND CO.

▲ CHINATOWN HERITAGE CENTRE

sized paper safes, servants and Mercedes for the self-respecting ghost about town.

### The Chinatown Heritage Centre

48 Pagoda St. Daily 10am–7pm. $8. The excellent Chinatown Heritage Centre offers a window on the district's cultural and mercantile past. Housed in three superbly restored shophouses, the centre is an invaluable social document, where the history, culture, pastimes and working life of Singapore's Chinese settlers spring to life. The museum is crammed with displays, artefacts and information boards, but it is also careful to give voice to former local residents, whose first-hand accounts of Chinatown life, projected onto walls at every turn, give a unique insight into the history of the Chinese in Singapore.

A model junk, like those on which early immigrants (*singkehs*) endured perilous journeys in search of work, sets the scene. Once ashore, settlers quickly formed clan associations or less savoury secret societies, and looked for employment. As you move through the centre's narrow corridors, these associations and societies, and every other facet of Chinatown life, work and leisure, are made flesh. All the while, you progress to a soundtrack of crashing gongs and cymbals, age-old songs of mourning and Fifties' crooners on scratchy 78s.

The genius of the centre lies in its detail, from the mock-up of the shabby flourishes of a prostitute's boudoir, and the marble table of a traditional coffee shop, to the pictures and footage of thin and haunted addicts seeking escape from the pain of their backbreaking work through opium, their "devastating master". The tour climaxes with a superb re-creation of the unbearable living quarters that settlers endured. Landlords were known to shoehorn forty tenants into a single floor; their cramped cubicles, cooking and bathing facilities are reproduced in all their grisly squalor. The absence of the cooling effect of any air-con goes some way towards conveying the stifling heat that residents daily suffered. There are sometimes walking tours of Chinatown based out of the centre; call ⓣ63252878 for details.

### Western Chinatown

Chinatown's main shopping drag comprises southbound New Bridge Road and northbound Eu Tong Sen Street, along which are found a handful of large malls. There are two striking buildings across the road from the *bak kwa* stalls at the intersection of Pagoda Street and New Bridge Road. Nearest is the flat-fronted Majestic Opera House, which no longer hosts performances but still boasts five images of Chinese opera stars over its doors. Just beside it, the Yue Hwa Chinese Products Emporium occupies the former *Great Southern Hotel*, which was built in 1927 by Eu Tong Sen, the son of Eu Yan Sang Medical Hall founder, Eu Kong. In its fifth-floor nightclub, *Southern Cabaret*, wealthy locals would drink liquor, smoke opium and pay to dance with so-called local "taxi girls." At the top of Eu Tong Sen Street, the beautiful, southern Chinese-style Thong Chai Medical Institute, with its wonderful serpentine gables and wooden inscribed pillars, has recently been listed as a national monument. The institute first opened its doors in 1892, with the avowed intention of dispensing free medical help regardless of race, colour or creed.

## Shops and markets

### Chinatown Complex

Sago St. Accessed up steps past garlic, fruit and nut hawkers, this teeming market's twists and turns reveal stalls selling silk, kimonos, rattan, leather, jade, tea, mah jong sets, Buddhist amulets and paraphernalia, and clothes. In the basement wet market, abacuses are still used to tally bills, and sugar canes lean like spears against the wall.

### Chu's Jade Centre

01-53/54 Chinatown Point, 133 New Bridge Rd. A gem of a store, specializing in semiprecious stones, huge clusters of freshwater pearl necklaces, and exquisite jade sculptures.

### Far East Inspirations

33 Pagoda St. **Far East Inspirations** is the classiest of several antique shops along Pagoda Street, offering Asian furniture, porcelain-based lamps, prints and watercolours.

▲ MAJESTIC OPERA HOUSE FACADE

▲ ZHEN LACQUER GALLERY

### House of Zhen

252 South Bridge Rd. Staff are friendly and knowledgeable at this expansive store, which carries a range of Asian antiques, collectables and furniture.

### Red Peach Gallery

68 Pagoda St. A fragrant shop, thanks to its soaps, candles, aromatherapy oils and incense; there are also contemporary Asian arts, housewares, and reproduction Ming dynasty furniture.

### Singapore Handicraft Centre

Chinatown Point, 133 New Bridge Rd. This place gathers around fifty souvenir and craft shops under one roof, making it a handy one-stop shopping point. Linen, jade, porcelain, tea sets, antique coins, opium pipes and cushions are just some of items you might pick up.

### Zhen Lacquer Gallery

1a/b Trengganu St. Specialists in boxes, bowls, trays and paintings, whose exquisite polished finish is crafted from the resin of the lacquer tree.

## Eating

### Ann Siang 5

5 Ann Siang Rd. Closed Sun. This civilized, cheery and airy café, just off trendy Club Street, serves scrambled eggs, Spanish omelettes and squidgy homemade cakes. Before you leave, check out the sumptuous Chinese-style dining rooms upstairs.

### Bak kwa stalls

203 & 207 New Bridge Rd. The smell produced by the *bak kwa* barbecue pork vendors, at the junction of Pagoda Street and New Bridge Road, as they cook their squares of red, fatty and delicious meat on wire meshes over fires, is pure Chinatown. Their *lap cheong* (Chinese sausage) is also good.

### Blue Ginger

97 Tanjong Pagar Rd ⓣ62223928. Housed in a renovated shophouse, this trendy but moderately priced Peranakan restaurant is a local favourite, thanks to dishes such as *ikan masal assam gulai* (mackerel simmered

▲ LAU PA SAT FESTIVAL MARKET

in a tamarind and lemongrass gravy), and that benchmark of Nonya cuisine, *ayam buah keluak* – braised chicken with Indonesian black nuts.

### Broth

21 Duxton Hill ☎63233353. Closed Sat lunch and all day Sun. The prices are reasonable and the fusion cuisine superb at this charming converted shophouse, an oasis on a delightfully quiet, tree-shaded Chinatown back street. The grilled threadfin fillet is tasty, and the Caesar salad to die for.

### China Square Food Centre

Telok Ayer St. *China Square Food Centre* houses three floors of spick-and-span stalls – mainly Chinese but with Japanese, Korean and Western representation. Choose from noodles, rice-based dishes, curries, juices and fruits, take a seat and tuck in.

### Chinese Opera Teahouse

5 Smith St ☎63234862. Fri & Sat only. The Sights and Sounds of Chinese Opera Show ($35), a set Chinese dinner serenaded by Chinese musicians, and followed by excerpts from Chinese operas performed by singers in full traditional garb, is a memorable cultural treat. Dinner begins at 7pm, though if you don't want a full meal you can watch the show while drinking tea and munching on Chinese snacks ($20); you'll be admitted at 7.50pm.

### Indochine

49 Club St ☎63230503. Closed Sun. *Indochine* is one of Singapore's most elegant restaurants, its beautiful Asian fixtures (Buddha effigies, stools, paintings) complemented by a truly great menu – pricey, but worth it – embracing Vietnamese, Lao and Cambodian cuisine. Try the Laotian *larb kai* (spicy chicken salad) or Nha Trang roast duck and mango salad. The Vietnamese *chao tom* (minced prawn wrapped round sugar cane) is also mouthwatering.

### Lau Pa Sat Festival Market

18 Raffles Quay. Daily 24hr. Dating to 1884, the octagonal, cast-iron-framed Lau Pa Sat Festival Market is the most atmospheric selection of hawker stalls in Singapore. As well as a range of Southeast Asian cuisine (though at slightly higher prices

than the norm), it offers free entertainment such as local bands and Chinese opera. At lunchtime the place is full to bursting with suits from the city, while late at night the clubbers take over. After 7pm, the portion of Boon Tat Street between Robinson Road and Shenton Way is closed to traffic, and traditional satay stalls and other hawker stalls take over the street.

### Maxwell Food Centre

Junction of South Bridge Rd and Maxwell Rd. An old-style hawker centre, a stone's throw from the centre of Chinatown, *Maxwell* serves no-frills, mostly Chinese fast food at its cheapest and most basic.

### Mitzi's

24–26 Murray Terrace ☎62220929. The cracking Cantonese food in this simple place, situated in a row of restaurants known as "Food Alley", draws crowds, so be prepared to queue. Two can eat for $30, plus drinks.

### Moi Kong Hakka Restaurant

22 Murray Terrace ☎62217758. The food of the semi-nomadic Hakka tribe relies heavily on salted and preserved ingredients. The inexpensive dishes here, at the best Hakka food outlet in Singapore, include red wine prawns and stewed pork belly with preserved vegetables.

### Moti Mahal Restaurant

18 Murray St ☎62214338. It's not cheap, but critics have voted *Moti Mahal* one of Singapore's very best Indian restaurants for years. The special is *murg massalam*, a whole chicken stuffed with rice (which needs to be ordered in advance).

### Mouth Restaurant

02-01 Chinatown Point, 133 New Bridge Rd ☎65344233. Daily 11am–4am. Beside the popular Hong Kong dim sum menu (served 11.30am–5pm), this jam-packed restaurant offers classy Cantonese food at under $20 a head.

### Swee Kee

*Damenlou Hotel*, 12 Ann Siang Rd ☎62211900. A Cantonese restaurant with real pedigree: Tang Swee Kee hawked the first bowl of his trademark *ka shou* fish-head noodles more than sixty years ago, and now his son sells this and other well-cooked

▲ MAXWELL FOOD CENTRE

▲ TEA CHAPTER

dishes from the attractive coffee shop on the ground floor of his Chinatown hotel.

### Tea Chapter

9a–11a Neil Rd. Daily 11am–11pm. One of a number of traditional teahouses along Neil Road, sup Chinese tea here, and you can sit in the very chair in which Queen Elizabeth sat when she visited in 1989. If you buy a bag of tea, the staff will teach you all the attached rituals; 100g bags cost from $5 to over $65, and tea sets are also on sale.

### Ya Kun Kaya Toast

01-01 Far East Square, 18 China St. Mon–Fri 7.30am–7pm, Sat & Sun 9am–5pm. This Hainanese joint started out as a Chinatown stall in 1944, and still offers a stirring start to the day: piping-hot, strong coffee with *kaya* toast – a slab of butter and a splodge of egg and coconut spread oozing from folded toast.

## Bars

### Backstage Bar

13a Trengganu St ☎62271712. Daily 7pm–2am. Sassy, red-walled gay bar plastered with posters of *The Sound of Music* and other musicals, and with a small balcony over the hustle and bustle of Chinatown where smokers go for a quick ciggie.

### Bar Savanh

49 Club St ☎63230145. Mon–Thurs 5pm–2am, Fri & Sat 5pm–3am, Sun 5pm–1am. You know a bar means business when it counts a six-metre waterfall and a koi carp pond among its fixtures and fittings. Candle-lit, and crammed with Buddha effigies, scatter cushions and plants, the *Savanh* (the name means "Heaven" in Lao) is a chilled-out bar if ever there was one, with cool acid-jazz sounds rounding things off nicely. Happy hour is 5pm to 8pm, and upstairs is sister establishment, the *Indochine* restaurant (p.92).

# The CBD and Boat Quay

**The mind-boggling ring of skyscrapers around Raffles Place form the epicentre of the Central Business District (CBD), Singapore's commercial heart. To the east, the mouth of the Singapore River features one of the island's flagship hotels, the *Fullerton*, and the Merlion statue – perhaps the island's most-photographed sight. West of the CBD, the river sweeps inland in a grand, "elephant's trunk" curve. Once clogged with bumboats carrying cargo to its godowns (warehouses), the river is now quieter and cleaner, and the former shophouses that line its banks have been to converted into fashionable bars and restaurants. Chugging a cold beer here, and viewing the CBD's spires reflected in the glassy water, is one of Singapore's most enjoyable experiences. From Raffles Place MRT, paths run along Boat Quay and beyond – though taking the same trip by river taxi (see p.159) is both more leisurely, and more memorable.**

## Raffles Place

Singapore's equivalent of Wall Street, Raffles Place is ringed by buildings so tall that pedestrians crossing the square feel like ants in a canyon. For the most striking way to experience its giddy heights, surface from Raffles Place MRT, follow the signs for Raffles Place itself out of the station, and gaze up towards the gleaming towers, blue skies and racing clouds. To your left is the soaring metallic triangle of the OUB Centre (Overseas Union Bank) and, to its right, the rocket-shaped UOB Plaza 2 (United Overseas Bank); in front of you are the rich brown walls of the former Standard Chartered Bank (now Six Battery Road), and to your right rise sturdy Singapore Land Tower and the almost Art Deco Caltex House. A smallish statue, entitled *Progress and Advancement*, stands at the northern end of Raffles Place. Erected in 1988, it's a miniature version of what was then the skyline of central

▲ RAFFLES PLACE

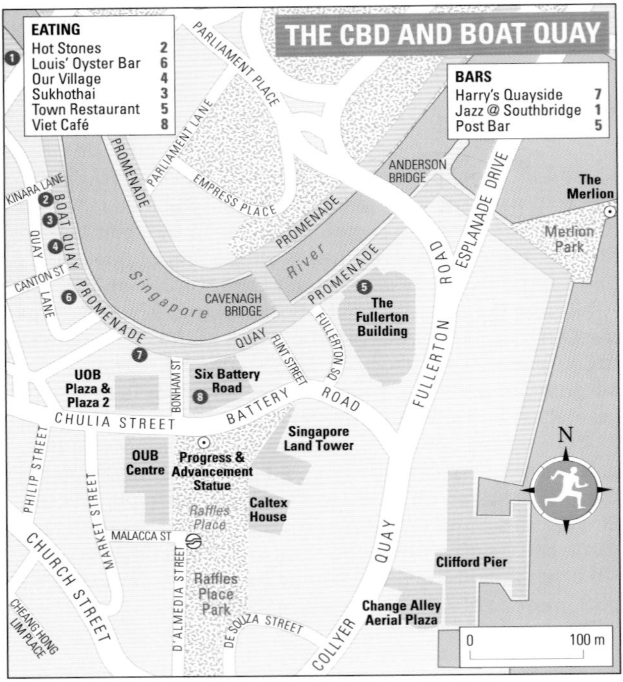

## THE CBD AND BOAT QUAY

**EATING**

| | |
|---|---|
| Hot Stones | 2 |
| Louis' Oyster Bar | 6 |
| Our Village | 4 |
| Sukhothai | 3 |
| Town Restaurant | 5 |
| Viet Café | 8 |

**BARS**

| | |
|---|---|
| Harry's Quayside | 7 |
| Jazz @ Southbridge | 1 |
| Post Bar | 5 |

Singapore. Inevitably, the very progress and advancement it celebrates has already rendered it out of date – not featured, for instance, is the UOB Plaza, a vast monolith of a building only recently built beside its twin, the UOB Plaza 2.

▲ THE FULLERTON BUILDING

## The Fullerton Building

▲ THE MERLION

The elegant, Neoclassical Fullerton Building, fronted by sturdy pillars, was built in 1928 at a cost of $4m as the headquarters for the General Post Office – a role it fulfilled until the mid-1990s. Remarkably, at the time, it was Singapore's tallest building – hence the lighthouse that still sits upon the roof. Old photographs of Singapore depict Japanese soldiers marching past after the surrender of the Allied forces during World War II; after the war ended, election campaign rallies were often addressed from its front steps. These days, the Fullerton Building is a luxury hotel, and the lighthouse a swanky restaurant.

## The Merlion

A huge statue of Singapore's national symbol, the Merlion, guards the mouth of the Singapore River. Half-lion, half-fish, and wholly ugly, the creature reflects the provenance of Singapore's name and its historical links with the sea – *Singapura* means "Lion City" in Sanskrit, after the Malay legend of a Sumatran prince who saw a lion on the island while sheltering from a storm. Adjacent Merlion Park (really little more than a concrete promontory) attracts tourists in their coachloads for its views of the mythical beast, and of the Theatres on the Bay across the river mouth.

## Boat Quay

It is no coincidence that the banks and finance houses of the CBD sprung up at the mouth of the Singapore River: with its trading companies, godowns and bumboats crammed with coffee, sugar and rice, the river formed the backbone of the island's mercantile growth for well over a century. With the development of the Port of Singapore, out west beyond Chinatown, however, the river went into decline. The area remained derelict until the early Nineties, when the 300-metre stretch of restored shophouses that constitutes Boat Quay was revitalized. It now boasts one of Singapore's highest concentrations of restaurants and bars. For the classic Boat Quay dining experience, choose a riverside table, from where you can best enjoy the vista of belanterned taxi boats, and the the lights from the opposite river bank dancing on the water – all framed by the high rises of Raffles Place towering overhead.

# Eating

### Hot Stones

53 Boat Quay ⓣ65345188. *Hot Stones* represents a healthy and novel twist on dining: steaks, chicken and seafood are grilled at table on squares of non-porous Alpine rock heated to 200°C – no oil or fat, but bags of flavour. Call ahead to book one of the handful of tables out front on the river bank.

### Louis' Oyster Bar

36 Boat Quay ⓣ65330534. Mon–Fri 11am–1am, Sat & Sun 5pm–3am. The Louis in question is Louis Armstrong, who beams down from all the walls. Oysters cost around $18 per half-dozen, and the "High Society Platter" (crayfish, crab, mussels, oysters and prawns on ice) is hard to resist.

### Our Village

5th floor, 46 Boat Quay ⓣ65383092. Closed Sat & Sun lunch. A hidden gem, with cheap but fine north Indian and Sri Lankan food, and peachy views of the river, city and colonial district from its charming, lamp-lit roof terrace. Try the rich *murgh makhanwala* (butter chicken) or the *malai kofta* (balls of paneer in a rich sauce), and finish with a palate-cleansing masala tea.

### Sukhothai

47 Boat Quay ⓣ65382422. Closed Sat & Sun lunch. Chef's recommendations at this Thai place include fried cotton fish topped with sliced green mangoes, but you can't go far wrong whatever you plump for from the extensive menu; the dining room is plain, so take advantage of the riverside tables.

### Town Restaurant

*Fullerton Hotel*, 1 Fullerton Square ⓣ67338388. Sun–Thurs 6.30am–midnight, Fri & Sat 6.30am–1am. Despite the eclectic range of moderately priced Asian and Western dishes on the menu, your best bet is a set meal from the barbecue, or the Saturday

▲ BOAT QUAY

▲ POST BAR, THE FULLERTON

Asian buffet lunch. Leather tub chairs and well-buffed pillars make for a refined atmosphere indoors, but for great river views, opt to eat out on the terrace.

### Viet Café

6 Battery Road, ☎62202186. Mon-Fri 11am–9pm. The heady mint, basil and citrus aromas of Vietnamese *pho* (soup) hang heavy in the air over the white banquettes and darkwood tables at sleek *Viet Café*. Choose from beef, chicken or seafood *pho* sets ($18), or try a Vietnamese dry vermicelli set meal ($15).

## Bars

### Harry's Quayside

28 Boat Quay. Daily 11am–1am. There's live jazz from Tuesday to Saturday in this upmarket place, and a blues jam every Sunday evening. The menu offers pasta, steaks and burgers, and drinks prices are lower in the early evening.

### Jazz @ Southbridge

82b Boat Quay ☎63274671. Sun–Thurs 11am–1am, Fri & Sat 11am–2am. The crowd here can be rather self-consciously jazzy (think polo necks and goatees), and the decor is rather muted, but there's no faulting the quality of the nightly live music sessions.

### Post Bar

*Fullerton Hotel*, 1 Fullerton Square. The "refrigeration shelf" running around the island bar in this slick hotel boozer ensures icy drinks from first swig to last, and the Merlion cocktail, with passion fruit liqueur and vodka, hits the spot.

# Little India

**A tour around Little India amounts to an all-out assault on the senses. Indian pop music blares from gargantuan speakers outside CD shops, the air is perfumed with incense, spices and jasmine garlands, Hindu women promenade in bright sarees, and a wealth of "hole-in-the-wall" restaurants serve up superior curries. Little India's roots date back to the first half of the nineteenth century when brick kilns and cattle farms were first established here. These drew so many Indian immigrants in search of work, that by the 1880s, the area was home to a thriving Indian community. The district's backbone is the northeast–southwest Serangoon Road, whose southern end is alive with shops, restaurants, temples and fortune-tellers. To the east, stretching as far as Jalan Besar, is a tight knot of roads whose shops and bustle make them good grounds for exploration, while parallel to Serangoon Road to the west, Race Course Road boasts a clutch of fine Indian restaurants and a noteworthy Buddhist temple.**

## Serangoon Road

Dating from 1822, and thus one of the island's oldest roadways, Serangoon Road is a kaleidoscopic whirl of Indian life, its shops selling everything from nose studs and ankle bracelets to incense sticks and *kum kum* powder (used to make the red dot Hindus wear on their foreheads). Little stalls, set up in doorways and under five-foot ways, sell garlands, gaudy posters of Hindu gods and gurus, movie soundtracks and newspapers such as *The Hindu* and *India Today*. Look out for parrot-wielding fortune-tellers – you tell the man

▲ FLOWER GARLANDS ON SALE, SERANGOON ROAD

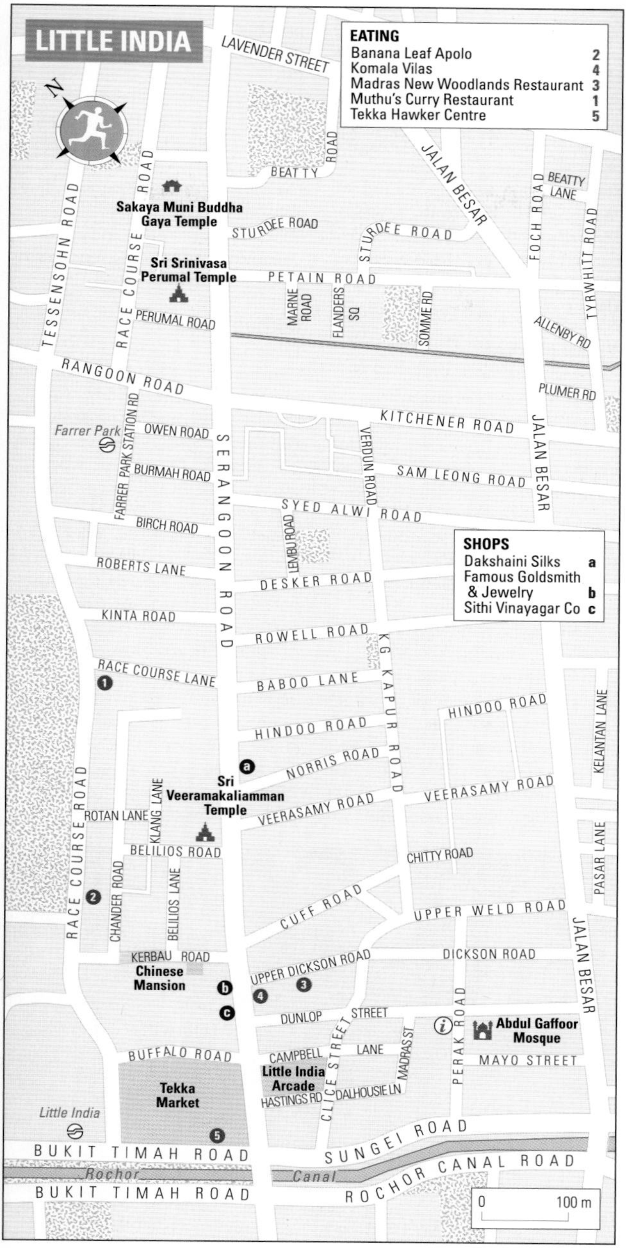

# LITTLE INDIA

**EATING**

| | |
|---|---|
| Banana Leaf Apolo | 2 |
| Komala Vilas | 4 |
| Madras New Woodlands Restaurant | 3 |
| Muthu's Curry Restaurant | 1 |
| Tekka Hawker Centre | 5 |

**SHOPS**

| | |
|---|---|
| Dakshaini Silks | a |
| Famous Goldsmith & Jewelry | b |
| Sithi Vinayagar Co | c |

N

LAVENDER STREET
BEATTY ROAD
JALAN BESAR
BEATTY LANE
FOCH ROAD
TYRWHITT ROAD
**Sakaya Muni Buddha Gaya Temple**
TESSENSOHN ROAD
RACE COURSE ROAD
STURDEE ROAD
**Sri Srinivasa Perumal Temple**
PETAIN ROAD
MARNE ROAD
FLANDERS SQ
SOMME RD
PERUMAL ROAD
ALLENBY RD
RANGOON ROAD
PLUMER RD
KITCHENER ROAD
Farrer Park
OWEN ROAD
FARRER PARK STATION RD
BURMAH ROAD
SERANGOON ROAD
VERDUN ROAD
SAM LEONG ROAD
JALAN BESAR
SYED ALWI ROAD
BIRCH ROAD
LEMBU ROAD
ROBERTS LANE
DESKER ROAD
KINTA ROAD
ROWELL ROAD
KG KAPUR ROAD
RACE COURSE LANE
BABOO LANE
HINDOO ROAD
HINDOO ROAD
KELANTAN LANE
NORRIS ROAD
**Sri Veeramakaliamman Temple**
VEERASAMY ROAD
VEERASAMY ROAD
RACE COURSE ROAD
ROTAN LANE
KLANG LANE
PASAR LANE
BELILIOS ROAD
CHITTY ROAD
CHANDER ROAD
BELILIOS LANE
CUFF ROAD
UPPER WELD ROAD
JALAN BESAR
KERBAU ROAD
**Chinese Mansion**
UPPER DICKSON ROAD
DICKSON ROAD
DUNLOP STREET
CLIVE STREET
MADRAS ST
PERAK ROAD
**Abdul Gaffoor Mosque**
BUFFALO ROAD
CAMPBELL LANE
MAYO STREET
**Little India Arcade**
HASTINGS RD
DALHOUSIE LN
**Tekka Market**
Little India
SUNGEI ROAD
BUKIT TIMAH ROAD
Rochor Canal
ROCHOR CANAL ROAD
BUKIT TIMAH ROAD
0 100 m

your name, he passes your name onto his feathered partner, and the bird then picks out a card with your fortune on it. Just off Serangoon Road, on Campbell Lane, you can't miss the riotously colourful flower shops where staff thread jasmine, roses and marigolds into garlands, or *jothi*, for prayer offerings. And a little further north, at 2 Cuff Rd, traditional spice grinders still ply their trade.

## Tekka Market

Serangoon Rd. Daily 8am–8pm. The Tekka Market, at the southern end of Serangoon Road, combines many of Little India's commercial elements under one roof. Beyond its ground-floor food centre is a wet market that's not for the faint-hearted – traders push around trolleys piled high with goats' heads, while the halal butchers go to work in full view of the customers. Elsewhere, live crabs shuffle busily in buckets, their claws tied together, and there's a mouthwatering range of fruits on sale, including mangoes and whole branches of bananas. Upstairs, on the second floor, you'll find Indian fabrics, leatherware, footwear, watches, and cheap electronic goods. On Sunday, the forecourt of the centre becomes an ad hoc social club for immigrant labourers working in Singapore, most of whom are Bangladeshi. Along the northern side of the market, Buffalo Road has a cluster of provisions stores selling Ayurvedic medicines, incense sticks, sacks of spices and fresh coconut, ground using a primitive machine out on the road.

## Kerbau Road

Little India's remaining shophouses are fast being touched up from the same pastel paintbox that has "restored" Chinatown to its present doll's house tweeness. Fortunately, the colours work far better in an Indian context, and the results are really quite pleasing. In particular, check out Kerbau Road, one block north of Buffalo Road, where shophouses have been meticulously renovated and now harbour a proliferation of Indian produce stores. If the mood takes you, you can get your hands painted with intricate henna patterns at Traditional Body Charm at no. 9; while Ansa, at no. 27, is a traditional Indian picture-framer's shop, packed with images of colourful

▲ TEKKA MARKET

▲ ABDUL GAFFOOR MOSQUE

Hindu deities. Look out, too, for the curving staircase, dragon-headed banisters and carved shutters of the old Chinese mansion at no. 37 – pop into TM Silks on the ground floor, and you can still see Chinese scenes painted high up on the walls and oriental beams finished with floral motifs.

## Little India Arcade

Daily 10am–9pm. Bounded by Serangoon Road to the west, Campbell Lane to the north, and Hastings Road to the south, the lovingly restored block of shophouses comprising Little India Arcade was opened a few years back as a sort of Little India in microcosm: behind its lime walls and green shutters you can purchase textiles and tapestries, bangles, religious statuary, Indian sweets, tapes and CDs, and even traditional Ayurvedic medicines. At the time of Deepavali, the arcade's narrow ways are choked with locals hastening to buy decorations, garlands, traditional confectionery and fine clothes.

## Abdul Gaffoor Mosque

41 Dunlop St. Daily 8.30am–noon & 2.30–4pm. Set amid gardens of palms and bougainvillea, the beautiful Abdul Gaffoor Mosque, with its green dome and bristling minarets, has enjoyed a comprehensive and sympathetic renovation in the last few years. Within its cream walls decorated with stars and crescent moons, the mosque features an unusual sundial over the entrance to the main prayer hall, its face ringed by elaborate Arabic script denoting the names of 25 Islamic prophets. Staff will give you a sarong or headdress to enable you to enter the prayer hall and see the mihrab, or arched niche where the imam sits, and the *mimbar*, or raised pulpit, from where he preaches. Traditionally, the imam always preaches from the second step of the *mimbar* as the top step is symbolically reserved for the prophet Mohammed.

## Sri Veeramakaliamman Temple

Opposite the turning to Veerasamy Rd, Serangoon Rd. 6am–noon & 4–9pm.

▲ HINDU WORSHIPPER AT THE SRI VEERAMAKALIAMMAN TEMPLE

Right in the heart of Little India, the Sri Veeramakaliamman Temple – dedicated to Kali, the ferocious Hindu goddess of power and incarnation of Lord Shiva's wife – features a fanciful *gopuram* that's flanked by majestic lions on the temple walls. The bells hanging on the temple doors are for worshippers – hoping their prayers will be answered – to ring as they enter. Inside, the *mandapam*, or worship hall, holds a jet-black image of Kali, depicted with a club in hand; flanking here are her sons, Ganesh and Murugan. Each year during Deepavali, a pulsating market takes place on the open land north of the temple.

## Sri Srinivasa Perumal Temple

397 Serangoon Rd. Daily 6am–noon & 4–9pm. At the edge of Little India, just west off Serangoon Road, the Sri Srinivasa Perumal Temple is dedicated to Lord Perumal, the Preserver of the Universe and god of mercy. The temple exterior features a five-tiered *gopuram*, with sculptures of the various manifestations of Lord Vishnu the Preserver. On the wall to the right of the front gate is a sculpted elephant, its leg caught in a crocodile's mouth.

Each year on the day of the Thaipusam festival, the temple courtyard witnesses a gruesome melee of activity, as Hindu devotees don huge metal frames (*kavadis*) topped with peacock feathers, which are fastened to their flesh with hooks and prongs. Stopping only while a coconut is smashed at their feet for good luck, the devotees then parade all the way to the Chettiar Temple south of Orchard Road on Tank Road.

## Sakaya Muni Buddha Gaya Temple

366 Race Course Rd. Daily 7am–6pm. Just northwest of the Sri Srinivasa Perumal Temple along a small path, the Sakaya Muni Buddha Gaya Temple (or Temple of the Thousand Lights) is a slightly kitsch building that betrays a strong Thai influence – not surprising, since it was built entirely by a Thai monk, Vutthisasala. On the left of the temple as you enter is a huge replica of the Buddha's footprint, inlaid with mother-of-pearl, beyond which is a 300-ton, 15m-high Buddha ringed by the thousand electric lights

from which the temple takes its alternative name; twenty-five scenes from the Buddha's life decorate the pedestal on which he sits. It is possible to walk inside the statue, through a door in its back – inside is a smaller representation of the Buddha, this time reclining. The left wall of the temple features a sort of wheel of fortune – to discover what lies in store, spin it (for 30¢) and take the numbered sheet of paper that corresponds to the number at which the wheel stops. Further along the left wall, a small donation entitles you to a shake of a tin full of numbered sticks, after which, again, you get a corresponding sheet of forecasts.

## Shops

### Dakshaini Silks

164 Serangoon Rd. Dakshaini stocks premier Indian embroidered silks and sarees. Some of the best lengths of silk are shot with gold or silver thread and sold by weight.

### Famous Goldsmith & Jewelry

91 Serangoon Rd. Bling, Indian-style, is the theme at this old shophouse, which stocks a large range of gold chains and jewellery.

### Sithi Vinayagar Co.

69 Serangoon Rd. This colourful store is stacked high with rolls of raw Thai and embroidered silks and bundles of sarees.

## Eating

### Banana Leaf Apolo

56–58 Race Course Rd ☎62938682. Daily 7am–10pm. Everything is served on banana leaves at this pioneering fish-head curry restaurant ($30 for two), where there's a delicious selection of spicy south Indian dishes. It's cheap and all-you-can-eat too – make sure to fold over your banana leaf when you're full, or you'll be given another dollop of rice and curry from the roving waiters.



▼ SHOPPING ON SERANGOON ROAD

▲ BANANA-LEAF THALI AT *KOMALA VILAS*

### Komala Vilas

76–78 Serangoon Rd ☎62936980. A popular and cramped vegetarian establishment specializing in *dosai*, which are served in fifteen different ways. The "South Indian Meal", served on a banana leaf, is great value at $12.

### Madras New Woodlands Restaurant

12–14 Upper Dickson Rd ☎62971594. Daily 7.30am–11.30pm. Functional, canteen-style place serving up decent vegetarian food at bargain prices. House specialities are the thali set meals; samosas, bhajis and other snacks are available after 3pm, and there's a big selection of sweets, too.

### Muthu's Curry Restaurant

76–78 Race Course Rd ☎62932389. Daily 10am–10pm. Recent renovations have greatly spruced up this south Indian restaurant. There's no menu, but it's famous for its fish-head curry ($16–25).

### Tekka Hawker Centre

Corner of Bukit Timah and Serangoon roads. Daily 8am–8pm. Predictably enough, Indian stalls are in the majority at this buzzing outdoor hawker centre – lunch at one of several biriyani stalls, and you won't need to eat again for the day. Chinese and Malay dishes are also available, if curry doesn't appeal.

# The Arab Quarter

**While Little India is memorable for its fragrances, you may find that it's the vibrant colours of the Arab Quarter that stick longest in the memory. The focal point of Singapore's Muslim population since Sir Stamford Raffles designated the area as an Islamic enclave in the 1820s, today the quarter is a riot of vivid sarongs, extravagantly painted shophouses, and golden breads and curries. Its defining landmarks are the golden dome of the Sultan Mosque, and the Istana Kampong Glam, a former royal palace that is now the site of the Malay Heritage Centre. The Arab Quarter has always had a strong mercantile tradition, and this finds its focus in Arab Street, Singapore's most famous destination for silks, batiks and other cloths. But if textiles are much in evidence, so is good Muslim food – be it Malay, North Indian or Arabic. Bounded by Arab Street, Beach Road, Jalan Sultan and Rochor Canal Road – and increasingly hemmed in by skyscrapers and shopping centres – the Arab Quarter is easily walkable in an hour.**

## The Sultan Mosque

3 Muscat St. Mon–Thurs & Sat 9am–1pm & 2–4pm, Fri 9–11.30am and 2.30–4pm. The Sultan Mosque, or Masjid Sultan, is the beating heart of the Muslim faith in Singapore – for the best initial views of its golden domes head to Baghdad Street and look north up Bussorah Street. Built on the site of an earlier nineteenth-century mosque and with the help of a $3000 donation from the East India Company, the present building was completed early in the last century to a design by colonial architects Swan and MacLaren: if you look carefully at the necks of the domes, you can see that the glistening effect is created by the reflection of the sun off the bases of thousands of ordinary glass bottles. Steps at the top of Bussorah Street lead past papaya and palm trees into a wide lobby, where a digital display lists

▲ PRAYER HALL, THE SULTAN MOSQUE

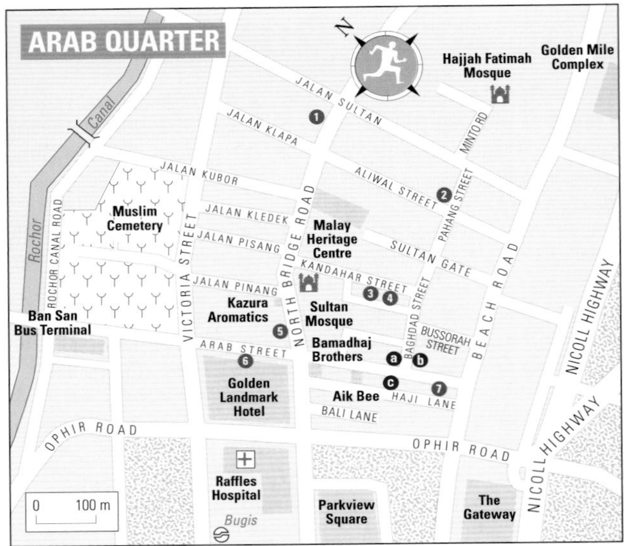


| EATING | | | | SHOPS | |
|---|---|---|---|---|---|
| Bumbu | 4 | Mooi Chin Palace Restaurant | 6 | Goodwill Trading Co | b |
| Café Le Caire | 7 | Rumah Makan Minang | 3 | Rishi Handicrafts | a |
| El Sheikh | 2 | Zam Zam Restaurant | 5 | S.S. Bobby Traders | c |
| Islamic Restaurant | 1 | | | | |

current prayer times; beyond, and out of bounds to non-Muslims, is the main prayer hall, a large, bare chamber that's fronted by two more digital clocks. The best time to experience life around the mosque is during the Muslim fasting month of Ramadan – the faithful can eat only after dusk, and Kandahar Street is awash with stalls selling biriyani, barbecued chicken and cakes.

▲ TEXTILE STORE, ARAB STREET

### Arab Street

An obstacle course of carpets, cloths, baskets and bags, Arab Street boasts the highest concentration of shops in the Arab Quarter. Most of these have been renovated, though one or two (such as Bamadhaj Brothers at no. 97 and Aik Bee at no. 73) still retain their original dark-wood and glass cabinets, and wide wooden benches where the shopkeepers sit. Textile stores are the most prominent along the street, their walls, ceilings and doorways draped with cloths and batiks, though you'll also see leather, basketware, gold, gemstones and jewellery for sale. It's easy to spend a couple of hours weaving in and out of the stores, but don't expect a quiet window-shopping session – the traders here are masters of the forced sale, and will have you loaded with sarongs, baskets and leather bags before you know it.

### North Bridge Road

The Arab Quarter's most evocative patch is the stretch of North Bridge Road between Arab Street and Jalan Sultan. Here, the men sport long sarongs and Abe Lincoln beards, the women fantastically colourful shawls and robes. Kazura Aromatics at 705 North Bridge Rd sells alcohol-free perfumes, while neighbouring shops stock rosaries, prayer mats, the *songkok* hats worn by Muslim males in mosques, and *miswak* sticks – twigs the width of a finger used by some locals to clean their teeth. There's also a gaggle of superb Muslim Indian restaurants.

### Malay Heritage Centre

Sultan Gate. Mon 1–6pm, Tues–Sun 10am–6pm; $3. Cultural show Wed 3.30pm & Sun 11.30am; $10. Squatting between Kandahar and Aliwal streets, the Malay Heritage Centre is housed within the Istana Kampong Glam. This modest colonial building was built as a palace for Sultan Ali Iskandar Shah, son of Sultan Hussein who negotiated with Raffles to hand over Singapore to the British in 1819; the sultan's descendants lived here until just a few years ago. The Heritage Centre displays various objects illustrating the history and culture of the Malay archipelago, including maps, model boats, cannons, ceremonial drums and daggers. The most engaging exhibits are upstairs, where touch screens cast light on Malay community life in the pre-war years of the twentieth century, and you can get a peek inside a mock-up of a traditional Malay kampung house. The centre's twice-weekly cultural show offers a passable blend of Malay music, dance and costumes.

### The Gateway

Beach Rd. The shops of Beach Road, just outside the Arab Quarter, betray its former proximity to the sea – there are ship's chandlers and fishing tackle

▲ THE GATEWAY BUILDING

specialists – but of greater note are the road's two logic-defying office buildings that together comprise The Gateway. Designed by I.M. Pei (who also designed the *Swissôtel* complex, see p.55), they rise magnificently into the air like vast razor blades and appear two-dimensional when viewed from certain angles. When Parkview Square, the huge, Gotham-esque building across Beach Road was built, much care was taken to site it dead between the Gateway's sharp, northwestward-pointing edges, so as to ward off bad feng shui. To be on the safe side, its developers placed four giant figures carrying good-luck pearls along the top of the tower.



### Hajjah Fatimah Mosque

Beach Rd. Daily 8.30am–noon & 2.30–4pm. Constructed in 1846, the Hajjah Fatimah Mosque was named after a wealthy Malaccan businesswoman who amassed a fortune through her mercantile vessels. The mosque's minaret looks strangely like a church steeple (perhaps because its architect was a European) and is beautifully illuminated at night; it has a six-degree list, leading to the mosque's local nickname – Singapore's Leaning Tower of Pisa.

### Golden Mile Complex

5001 Beach Rd. The Golden Mile Complex, across the road from the Hajjah Fatimah Mosque, attracts so many Thai nationals, particularly on Sundays, that locals refer to it as "Thai Village". Inside, the shops vend Thai foodstuffs, cafés sell Singha beer and Mekong whisky, and authentic restaurants serve up old favourites.

▲ MUSLIM MAN OUTSIDE HAJJAH FATIMAH MOSQUE

## Shops

### Goodwill Trading Co.

56 Arab St. Goodwill Trading specializes in Indonesian batik sarongs, which are heaped high on varnished wood shelves. The shop is noted especially for its excellent *pulicat* (plaid sarongs), favoured by Malay men.

### Rishi Handicrafts

58 Arab St. Leather sandals, necklaces, briefcases, belts and knick-knacks are all stocked at Rishi, alongside an impressive range of basketware and rattan work, including fans, hats and walking sticks.

### S.S. Bobby Traders

57 Arab St. Hanging textiles form a colourful curtain along the facade of this Arab Street shophouse. Indian, Chinese and Thai silks, linen and lace can be

▲ BASKET AND LEATHERWARE STORE, ARAB STREET

cut to length or sold as sarongs or table linen.

# Eating

### Bumbu

44 Kandahar St ☎63928628. Crammed with Singaporean antiques amassed by owner, Robert Tan, *Bumbu* is as much a social history museum as restaurant. Happily, the furnishings don't outshine the fine Indonesian/Thai cuisine on offer. The signature dish, crispy "fish pillow" – fish mixed with spices and deep fried – is worth the journey alone.

### Café Le Caire

39 Arab St ☎62920979. Daily 10am– late. This informal diner spearheaded the revival of Arab cuisine in the Arab Quarter, and remains a good inexpensive bet for Lebanese and Egyptian specialities as well as more obscure Saudi and Yemeni dishes. If you're into hubble-bubbles, take advantage of the huge range of tobaccos – they do over a dozen.

### El Sheikh

18 Pahang St ☎62969116. The menu at this excellent Lebanese restaurant runs the usual gamut, from *meze* (with plenty for vegetarians) to main courses such as *shish taouk* (filleted chicken on a skewer). Combination platters ($12) and mains (from $10) are both good value, there's a great selection of juices and desserts, and board games and flavoured hookahs are on offer too. Choose to sit either in the indoor dining areas or the terrace and garden.

### Islamic Restaurant

791–797 North Bridge Rd ☎62987563. Daily except Fri 9.30am–9.30pm. This aged Muslim restaurant, manned by a gang of old men who plod solemnly up and down between the tables, boasts the best chicken biriyani ($15 for two) in Singapore, cooked in the traditional way – heated from above and below with charcoal.

### Mooi Chin Palace Restaurant

*Golden Landmark Hotel*, Arab St ☎63921600. Hainanese immigrants often worked as domestics to colonial families, resulting in crossover dishes such as Hainanese mutton soup and Hainanese pork chop. Both are cooked to perfection here, where whole pomfret *sambal* ($25) is a speciality, and set menus start from around $30 for two. In addition to lunch and dinner, the restaurant is open 7.30–9am for dim sum.

### Rumah Makan Minang

18a Kandahar St. Cafeteria-style *nasi padang* restaurant, where customers choose at a buffet counter from a range of highly spiced Sumatran dishes; $4 ensures a good feed.

### Zam Zam Restaurant

699 North Bridge Rd. The main reason to come to this simple curry joint is to see the *murtabak* maker work his magic on the huge griddle out front (a *murtabak* is best described as an Indian bread pizza). In addition, *Zam Zam* also knocks out decent *rendang*s and biriyanis.

# Northern Singapore

**The varied attractions north of the city centre are spread across a fan-shape of land extending twenty kilometres up to the Straits of Johor and Peninsular Malaysia beyond. Desite its numerous sprawling, maze-like modern suburbs – Toa Payoh, Ang Mo Kio, Woodlands, Kranji – much of northern Singapore retains a rural feel. The principal draw, some 15km northwest of the Padang, is the beautifully landscaped Singapore Zoo, which, with its adjacent Night Safari, make for a full day-trip. Less manicured terrains still exist at Bukit Timah Nature Reserve, a stand of primary rainforest; on the trails and canopy walk around MacRitchie Reservoir; and at Sungei Buloh Wetland Reserve, which protects the island's mangrove ecosystem. Two sights, Kranji War Memorial and the new Memories at Old Ford Factory gallery, recall the battles fought in this part of the island by Allied and Japanese forces in 1942, while there are also two of Singapore's largest and most impressive temple complexes to explore. Travel in the north is by bus and MRT and often a combination of both.**

### Bukit Timah Nature Reserve

Ⓣ64685736, Ⓦwww.nparks.gov.sg. Daily 6.30am–7.30pm (visitor centre open daily 8.30am–6pm). Free. Bus #171 from Somerset or Scotts roads, or bus #170 from the Ban San terminal on Queen St. Bukit Timah Nature Reserve, an 81-hectare park some 8km north from the centre, represents Singapore's last remaining pocket of primary rainforest. The reserve is a refuge for the dwindling numbers of species – only 25 types of mammal, for example – that still exist on the island. Creatures you're most likely to see in Bukit Timah include long-tailed macaques, butterflies and other insects, and birds such as the dark-necked tailorbird, which builds its nest by sewing together leaves. Scorpions, snakes, flying lemurs and pangolins (anteaters, whose name is derived from the Malay word *peng-goling*, meaning "roller" – a reference to the animal's habit of rolling into a ball when threatened) still roam here too.

Begin your trip at the informative visitor centre, which is full of displays, specimens and photos relating to the reserve's flora and fauna. Several paths from the centre twist and turn through the forest around and to the top of Bukit Timah Hill which, although a paltry 163m, is actually Singapore's highest hill; the route up takes either 45 minutes or two hours depending on which trail you take. All the paths are all well signposted, colour coded and dotted with rest points, and they're clearly mapped on the free leaflet handed out to all visitors. Bike tracks

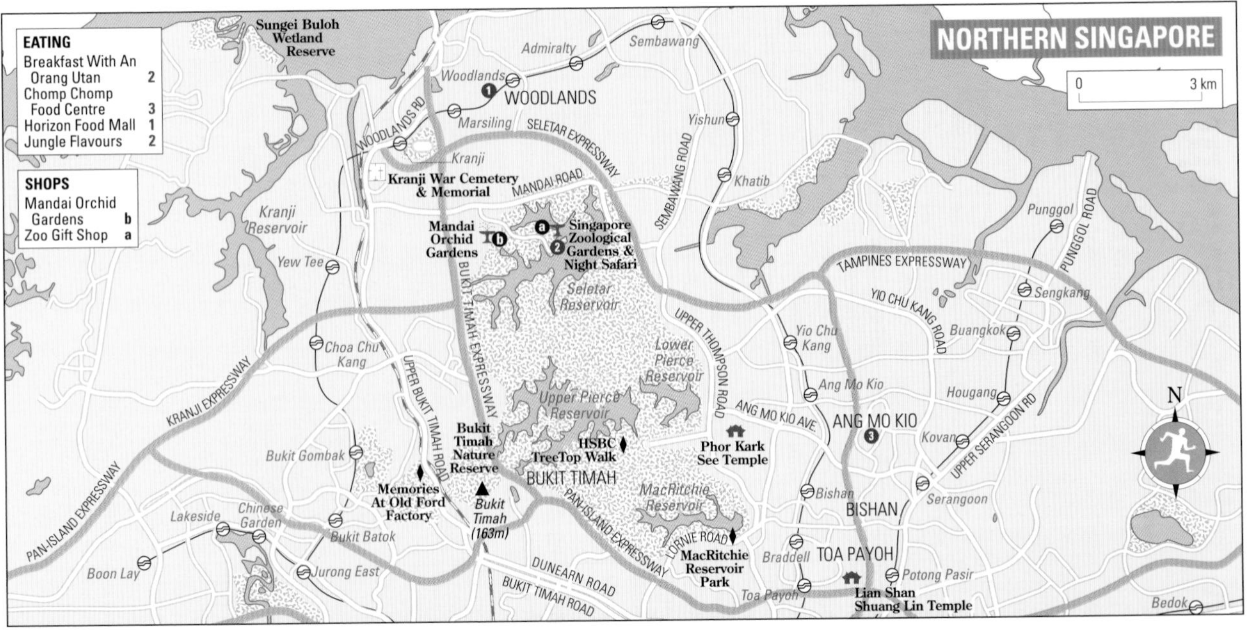
NORTHERN SINGAPORE
0
3 km
N
EATING
Breakfast With An Orang Utan 2
Chomp Chomp Food Centre 3
Horizon Food Mall 1
Jungle Flavours 2
SHOPS
Mandai Orchid Gardens b
Zoo Gift Shop a
Sungei Buloh Wetland Reserve
Admiralty
Sembawang
Woodlands
WOODLANDS
Marsiling
Yishun
WOODLANDS RD
SELETAR EXPRESSWAY
Kranji
Kranji War Cemetery & Memorial
MANDAI ROAD
SEMBAWANG ROAD
Khatib
Kranji Reservoir
Mandai Orchid Gardens
Singapore Zoological Gardens & Night Safari
Punggol
PUNGGOL ROAD
Yew Tee
TAMPINES EXPRESSWAY
Seletar Reservoir
Sengkang
YIO CHU KANG ROAD
Buangkok
UPPER THOMPSON ROAD
Yio Chu Kang
Choa Chu Kang
Lower Pierce Reservoir
BUKIT TIMAH EXPRESSWAY
UPPER BUKIT TIMAH ROAD
Ang Mo Kio
Hougang
KRANJI EXPRESSWAY
Upper Pierce Reservoir
ANG MO KIO AVE.
ANG MO KIO
Kovan
UPPER SERANGOON RD
Bukit Timah Nature Reserve
HSBC TreeTop Walk
Phor Kark See Temple
Bukit Gombak
BUKIT TIMAH
Memories At Old Ford Factory
Bukit Timah (163m)
MacRitchie Reservoir
Bishan
BISHAN
Serangoon
PAN-ISLAND EXPRESSWAY
Lakeside
Chinese Garden
Bukit Batok
LORNIE ROAD
MacRitchie Reservoir Park
Braddell
TOA PAYOH
Boon Lay
Jurong East
DUNEARN ROAD
BUKIT TIMAH ROAD
Toa Payoh
Potong Pasir
Lian Shan Shuang Lin Temple
Bedok

▲ MACAQUE, BUKIT TIMAH NATURE RESERVE

have also been added; mountain bikes can be hired from Bike & Hike, 382 Upper Bukit Timah Rd (Ⓣ67638382), for $6 an hour.

### Memories at Old Ford Factory

Upper Bukit Timah Rd. Mon–Fri 9am–5.30pm, Sat 9am–1.30pm. Free. Bus #171 from Somerset or Scotts roads, or bus #170 from Ban San Terminal on Queen St. This new gallery at the Art Deco old Ford car factory, tells the story of the Allied surrender to the Japanese, which took place here, and of the dark years of Japanese occupation from 1942 to 1945. The exhibition uses period newspapers and first-hand audio accounts to bring to life the civilian experience of occupation, with displays including relics such as Morse coders, anti-tank guns, signal lamps and grenades. The wartime garden behind the building has been planted with oil palm, tapioca, sweet potato, papaya and other food crops grown during the occupation.

▲ MEMORIES AT OLD FORD FACTORY

## The MacRitchie Trails and HSBC TreeTop Walk

MacRitchie Reservoir Park open daily 6.30am–7.30pm; free; bus #132, #166 or #167 from downtown and alight on Lornie Rd. HSBC TreeTop Walk open Tues–Fri 9am–5pm, Sat & Sun 8.30am–5pm; free. It's a 4km hike from the MacRitchie Reservoir Park to the TreeTop Walk, or take any of the buses listed above and alight at the turning to the Singapore Island Country Club on Upper Thomson Rd. The shoreline and environs of the MacRitchie Reservoir Park play host to the MacRitchie Trails, a network of six colour-coded tracks and boardwalks allowing you to experience Singapore's lowland tropical dipterocarp forest. All the trails start at MacRitchie Reservoir Park's visitor centre, where there are toilets, a café and information boards. Bisecting lush vegetation and skirting the reservoir's glassy waters, the trails offer the chance to see macaques, monitor lizards, terrapins, squirrels, eagles and kingfishers in the wild. On the second Sunday of the month a free nature appreciation walk starts from the head of the Prunus Trail at 9.30am (Ⓣ65545127 to pre-book).

One of the longer walks, the 10km Blue Trail, leads to the HSBC TreeTop Walk, a free-standing, 25m-high, 250m-long suspension bridge. Spanning the two highest points in the MacRitchie area – Bukit Kalang and Bukit Peirce – the bridge gives you a fine monkey's-eye view of the forest canopy.

▲ LIAN SHAN SHUANG LIN TEMPLE

## Lian Shan Shuang Lin Temple

184e Jalan Toa Payoh, Toa Payoh. Daily 7am–5pm. MRT to Toa Payoh station, from where the temple is a ten-minute walk. Established at the turn of the last century, the Lian Shan Shuang Lin Temple Complex (the name translates as "Twin Groves of the Lotus Mountain" – a reference to the Buddha's birth in a grove of trees and his death under a Bodhi tree) has retained its appeal despite several renovations. Set behind a half-moon pool, the temple is accessed by the Hall of Celestial Kings, where statues of the Four Kings of Heaven stand guard to repel evil, which is symbolized by the demons under their feet. The kings flank Maitreya Bodhisattva, the Laughing Buddha, believed to grant good luck if you rub his stomach. Beyond, a courtyard dotted with bonzai plants and lilies in dragon jars leads to the main Mahavira Hall, where a Sakyamuni Buddha in lotus position takes centre stage. To his right is the medicine Buddha, the great healing teacher, and to his left, the Amitabha Buddha.

Elsewhere in the compound is a grand hall with a 100-armed Kuan Yin, Goddess of Mercy, flanked by chandeliers; and the impressive seven-tiered Dragon Light Pagoda.

### Phor Kark See Temple

88 Bright Hill Drive, Bishan. Daily 7am–5pm. Bus #130 from Victoria St, alighting at the far end of Sin Ming Drive. The largest temple complex in Singapore lies north of MacRitchie Reservoir, right in the middle of the island. Phor Kark See Temple spreads over nineteen acres and combines temples, pagodas, pavilions, a Buddhist library and a vast crematorium – so impressive is the site, that it has been used several times as a backdrop to Chinese kung fu movies. Phor Kark See boasts none of the faded charm of Singapore's older temples, but relies instead on sheer magnitude and exuberant decor for its effect. Multi-tiered roofs bristle with ceramic dragons, phoenixes, birds and human figures, while around the complex are statues of various deities including a nine-metre-high marble statue of Kuan Yin and a soaring pagoda capped by a golden *chedi* (reliquary tower). A new prayer hall was inaugurated in early 2006, housing what is reputed to be the biggest seated Buddha in Southeast Asia.

▲ BUDDHA STATUE AT PHOR KARK SEE TEMPLE

### Singapore Zoological Gardens

Mandai Lake Rd, Ang Mo Kio Ⓦ www.zoo.com.sg. Daily 8.30am–6pm. $15, kids $7.50; $28/14 including Night Safari, $35/17.50 including Night Safari and Jurong BirdPark. Bus #171 to Mandai Rd, then #927, or go to Ang Mo Kio MRT and then take bus #138. Home to as huge and as apparently happy a population of animals as you'll ever see in captivity, the Singapore Zoological Gardens are spread over a promontory jutting into peaceful Seletar Reservoir. Moats are preferred to cages for many of the 3200 animals here, which represent more than 330 species. A tram ($5/2.50 for three stops) circles the grounds on a one-way circuit, but be prepared for a lot of footwork. Highlights include orang-utans, Komodo dragons and polar bears, which you view underwater from a gallery. Also worth checking out is the special loan enclosure that has played host to a giant panda, an Indian white tiger and a golden monkey. No exhibit lets you get any closer to the resident animals than the Fragile Forest biodome, a magical zone where you can walk amid ring-tailed lemurs, tree kangaroos, sloths and fruit bats. Various animal and feeding shows run throughout the day from 10am until 5pm, featuring sea lions, elephants, polar bears and other exotic creatures. There are also elephant ($6/3) and pony ($4) rides and, in the Children's World, the chance to hold young chicks and watch a milking demonstration.

### Night Safari

Singapore Zoological Gardens Ⓦwww.zoo.com.sg. Daily 7.30pm–midnight. $20, kids $10; $28/14 including zoo, $35/17.50 including zoo and Jurong BirdPark. At Singapore Zoo's Night Safari, a thousand animals representing well over a hundred species – amongst them, elephants, rhinos, giraffes, leopards, hyenas and otters – play out their nocturnal routines under a forest of standard lamps. Three walking trails, geared around – respectively – giant forest trees, leopards, and the incredibly cute fishing cats, wind through the safari. However, only five of the safari's eight zones can be explored on foot – to see the rest you'll need to take the 45-minute *Jurassic Park*-style tram ride ($8/4), and tolerate the intrusive chattering of its taped guide. A meal at one of the restaurants outside the entrance will pass the time between the zoo's closing and the safari's opening.

▲ SINGAPORE ZOOLOGICAL GARDENS

### Mandai Orchid Gardens

Mandai Lake Rd Ⓣ62691036, Ⓦwww.singaporeorchids.com.sg. Daily 8.30am–5.30pm; $3. A 10-minute walk from the Singapore Zoological Gardens or bus #138 from the zoo stops outside. Orchids are big business in tropical Singapore, and the Mandai Orchid Gardens make a brilliantly colourful detour on the way to or from the zoo. The flowers are cultivated on a gentle slope and tended by old ladies in wide-brimmed hats. As little effort has been taken to make the gardens instructive, you'll need to be a keen horticulturalist to get the most out of them. That said, wandering the long rows of blooms makes for a pleasing half-hour, and offers loads of scope for photography.

▲ MANDAI ORCHID GARDENS

## Kranji War Cemetery and Memorial

Woodlands Rd, Woodlands. Daily 7am–6pm. Bus #170 from Ban San Terminal on Queen St passes the cemetery, or it's a 500-metre walk from Kranji MRT. Only the peaceful sound of birds and insects breaks the silence at the immaculately kept grounds of Kranji War Cemetery and Memorial, the resting place of the many Allied troops who died in the defence of Singapore during World War II. As you enter, row upon row of graves slope up the landscaped hill in front of you, some

## Singapore and World War II

**Kranji War Cemetery**'s horrific scale underlines the huge loss of life incurred when Japanese forces under General Yamashita invaded Singapore, "the strongest British bastion east of Suez", in February 1942. By attacking from Malaya to the north, the Japanese remained out of range of the guns of **Fort Siloso**, which pointed south from what is now Sentosa Island. From its base on Fort Canning Hill (now the **Battle Box**), the Allied Command, led by Lieutenant-General Arthur Percival, tried to muster a defence of the island, and for a few days battles raged in the hills and jungle of north and west Singapore. One such battle took place at Pasir Panjang Village, where a brigade of Malays made a heroic 48-hour stand before being all but wiped out; their courage is remembered at **Reflections at Bukit Chandu**. Faced with further loss of life, Percival travelled to the **Ford Motor Factory** at Bukit Timah Village, where Yamashita was now based, and surrendered on Sunday, February 15.

The Japanese renamed Singapore *Syonan*, or "Light of the South", and three and a half years of brutal Japanese rule ensued, during which thousands of civilians were executed in vicious anti-Chinese purges, and Europeans were either marched up to work on Thailand's infamous "Death Railway", or herded into Changi Prison. The depravation suffered at Changi is starkly recalled at the **Changi Prison Museum**. Less well known is the vicious campaign, known as Operation Sook Ching, mounted by the military police, or *Kempeitai*, during which upwards of 25,000 Chinese males between 18 and 50 years of age were shot dead at Punggol and Changi beaches as enemies of the Japanese.

▲ GARDENERS AT KRANJI WAR CEMETERY.

identified only as “known unto God”. A simple stone cross stands over the cemetery, and above it looms the memorial, which records the names of more than twenty thousand soldiers – from Britain, Canada, Sri Lanka, India, Malaysia, the Netherlands, New Zealand and Singapore – who died in the region. Two unassuming tombs stand on the wide lawns below the cemetery, belonging to Yusof Bin Ishak and Dr Benjamin Henry Sheares, independent Singapore’s first two presidents.

## Sungei Buloh Wetland Reserve

Ⓣ67941401, Ⓦwww.sbwr.org.sg. Mon–Sat 7.30am–7pm, Sun 7am–7pm; Mon–Fri $1, children 50¢, Sat & Sun free. Free guided tours Sat 9am, 10am, 3pm & 4pm; pre-book at other times

▼ SUNGEI BULOH WETLAND RESERVE

($50 per group). MRT to Kranji MRT station, then bus #925; on Sun this stops at the reserve's entrance but Mon to Sat it only goes as far as Kranji Reservoir car park, from which it's a 15-minute walk to the reserve. The 130-hectare swathe of Sungei Buloh Wetland Reserve on Singapore's north coast is the island's only protected wetland nature area. Beyond its visitor centre, café and video theatre, which shows a 15-minute audiovisual overview explaining the park's ecosystem (9am–5pm: Mon–Sat every 2hr; Sun hourly), walking routes thread through an expanse of mangrove, mud flats, orchards and grassland. These are home to kingfishers, herons, sandpipers, kites and sea eagles and – in the waters – mudskippers, needlefish and archerfish, which squirt water to knock insects out of the air and into devouring range. The reserve's 500-metre-long mangrove boardwalk offers an easy means of getting a sense of the shoreline environment, and en route among the swamp's reaching fingers you'll spot tortoises and crabs. From here you can graduate to walks ranging from three to seven kilometres into the guts of the reserve. The best time to visit the park is between September and March, when you're likely to catch sight of migratory birds from around Asia roosting and feeding.

# Shops

### Mandai Orchid Gardens

Mandai Lake Rd. Once you've viewed the splendid blooms on display at the gardens, you'll find it hard to resist one of the gift boxes of orchids (from $20) available here. Prices compare favourably with those at florists downtown and at the airport.

### Zoo Gift Shop

Singapore Zoo, 80 Mandai Lake Rd. Set beside the zoo's entry gates, the gift shop offers bags of opportunities for gift purchases, from cuddly orang-utans to natural history books.

# Eating

### Breakfast With An Orang Utan

Singapore Zoo, 80 Mandai Lake Rd, ☎62693411. Daily 9–10am. At *Breakfast With An Orang Utan*, a bumper buffet-style spread with seasonal tropical fruits is shared with whichever orang is on duty ($15.50).

### Chomp Chomp Food Centre

20 Kensington Park Rd. Daily noon–midnight. Kovan MRT and take a taxi. Locally famed for its carrot cake, Hokkien fried *mee*, grilled *sambal* stringray and *satay bee hoon*, this sleepy food centre offers an enjoyable slice of local suburban life.

### Horizon Food Mall

Causeway Point, 1 Woodlands Sq, Woodlands. Daily 10.30am–10.30pm. Woodlands MRT. *Horizon* is a clean, busy local food centre with good Japanese, Malay and Indian stalls, and a safe bet if hunger pangs strike when you are in the far north of Singapore, en route to or from Sungei Buloh or Kranji cemetery.

### Jungle Flavours

Singapore Zoo, 80 Mandai Lake Rd. Daily 10am–6pm. The largest of the five outlets that together comprise the zoo's *Restaurants in the Wild* complex, self-service *Jungle Flavours* offers Asian, Oriental and Western snacks and meals.

# Eastern Singapore

**Across the Kallang Basin from the Arab Quarter, eastern Singapore has a mellow, sea-breezy ambience that provides a welcome foil to the airless downtown districts. Particularly rewarding to explore are the suburbs of Geylang and Katong, which maintain a strong Malay identity that comes alive in the shops and markets of Joo Chiat. To its south, man-made East Coast Park sweeps eastwards. By day it's dotted with sailing boats and windsurfers; by night, its restaurants do a roaring trade in chilli crab. Changi Village, at the eastern tip of the island, may have lent its name to the adjacent airport, but it remains synonynous with the infamous prison where the Japanese interned Allied troops and civilians – a period of history commemorated at Changi Museum. From Changi Point, bumboats run out to Pulau Ubin, a tiny island whose dirt tracks and stilt houses carry echoes of pre-development Singapore. Buses serve most of the attractions out this way, though Paya Lebar, Bedok and Tanah Merah MRT stations are also handy springboards.**

▲ PERANAKAN HOUSES, KOON SENG ROAD

## Joo Chiat

Joo Chiat Rd is a short walk from Paya Lebar MRT. There's no better place to get a sense of the atmosphere of the east than Joo Chiat district, in the adjoining eastern suburbs of Geylang and Katong. Malay culture and community have held sway here since the mid-nineteenth century, when Malays and Indonesians converged to work the coconut and lemongrass farms. Later, Peranakan (or Straits Chinese) families settled in the area in numbers; their architecture and cuisine remain evident today.

Signposting the start of the road is Joo Chiat Complex, where textile merchants drape their wares on any available floor and wall space, transforming the drab interior into a sort of Asian souk. More market than shopping centre, it's a prime destination for anyone interested in buying silk, batik, rugs, muslin or the traditional *baju kurung* worn by Malay women. Stalls around the perimeter of the complex sell dates, honey, Malay CDs and *jamu* (Malay medicine).

A stroll along Joo Chiat Road from the complex unearths shops, restaurants and architecture that showcase Singapore's Straits Chinese heritage. Joo Chiat Road itself has some beautifully restored shophouses, like Chiang Pow Joss Paper Trading at no. 252, where funerary paraphernalia is made beneath an elaborate facade of flowers and dragons. But to see the area's most immaculate Peranakan shophouses, you'll need to turn on to Koon Seng Road (on the east side, about halfway down Joo Chiat Road), where painstaking work has restored multicoloured facades, French windows, eaves and mouldings.

Back on Joo Chiat, several shops are worthy of a detour. Kway Guan Huat at no. 95 makes *popiah* skins for spring rolls, while mackerel *otah* (fish paste wrapped and steamed in banana leaf) is produced at no. 267. There are non-alcoholic perfumes and Arab CDs at Haruman Makkah at no. 142; and Malay medicines next door at Fatimah Trading.

### East Coast Park

East Coast Parkway Ⓦwww.nparks.gov.sg. Take bus #16 and alight at Marine Terrace, from where a pedestrian underpass will bring you into the park. The palm-shaded tracks, barbecue pits and beaches of East Coast Park draw Singaporeans in their droves. The entire park stands on reclaimed land – its clean sands were long ago transported in from elsewhere. Sunbathing is popular, but the emphasis is equally on physical activity, whether rollerblading, cycling (bikes can be rented for $4–8 per day; bring some ID), swimming or sailing.

### Changi Museum

Ⓣ62142451, Ⓦwww.changimuseum.com. Daily 9.30am–4pm. Free. Take bus #2 from Chinatown or Victoria St, or MRT to Tanah Merah station, and pick up the #2 there. Infamous Changi Prison was the site of a World War II POW camp in which Japanese jailers subjected Allied prisoners to the harshest of treatment. The prison is still in use, but its terrible past is marked in the hugely moving Changi Museum nearby. The museum's power lies in the many cruelties it portrays. Sketches, photographs and information boards plot the Japanese occupation of Singapore and the consequent fate of the soldiers and civilians incarcerated in camps around the Changi area. Look out, in particular, for the photographs of the camp and its inmates taken by George Aspinall and the replica artworks of W.R.M. Haxworth and Stanley Warren – the latter pair used camouflage paint, crushed snooker chalk and aircraft paints smuggled in by fellow POWs to paint Bible scenes on a Changi chapel wall. It's possible to get the merest sense of prison life by entering the Changi Cell, a dark, stuffy alleyway that approximates the cramped confinement suffered by POWs. Here, the voices of former prisoners recall enduring the "howling, crying, shouting" of fellow inmates being tortured in the middle of the night. Outside in a courtyard is a replica of a simple wooden chapel typical of those erected in Singapore's wartime camps; the brass cross on its altar was crafted from spent ammunition casings, while its walls carry more poignant messages of

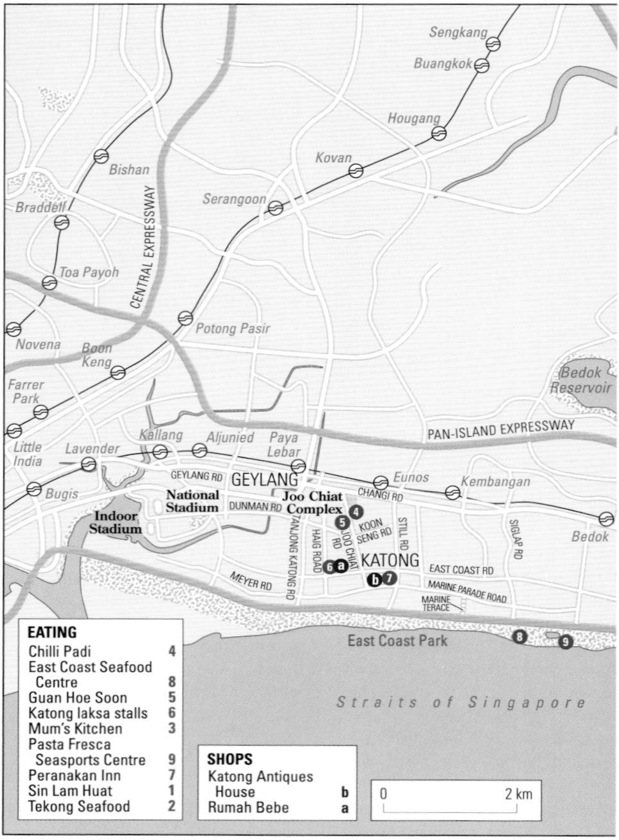

**EATING**

| | |
|---|---|
| Chilli Padi | 4 |
| East Coast Seafood Centre | 8 |
| Guan Hoe Soon | 5 |
| Katong laksa stalls | 6 |
| Mum's Kitchen | 3 |
| Pasta Fresca Seasports Centre | 9 |
| Peranakan Inn | 7 |
| Sin Lam Huat | 1 |
| Tekong Seafood | 2 |

**SHOPS**

| | |
|---|---|
| Katong Antiques House | b |
| Rumah Bebe | a |

▼ CELL DOOR, CHANGI PRISON MUSEUM

remembrance penned by visiting former POWs and relatives. Most moving of all, though, is the board of remembrance, where wives, children and compatriots have pinned messages for the dead.

## Pulau Ubin

Bus #2 to Changi Point, then catch a bumboat from the left-hand jetty. Boats leave when full; $2 each way; 10min.

Pulau Ubin, 2km off Changi Point in the Straits of Johor, gives an idea of what Singapore would have been like fifty years ago. The island is just 7km by 2km,

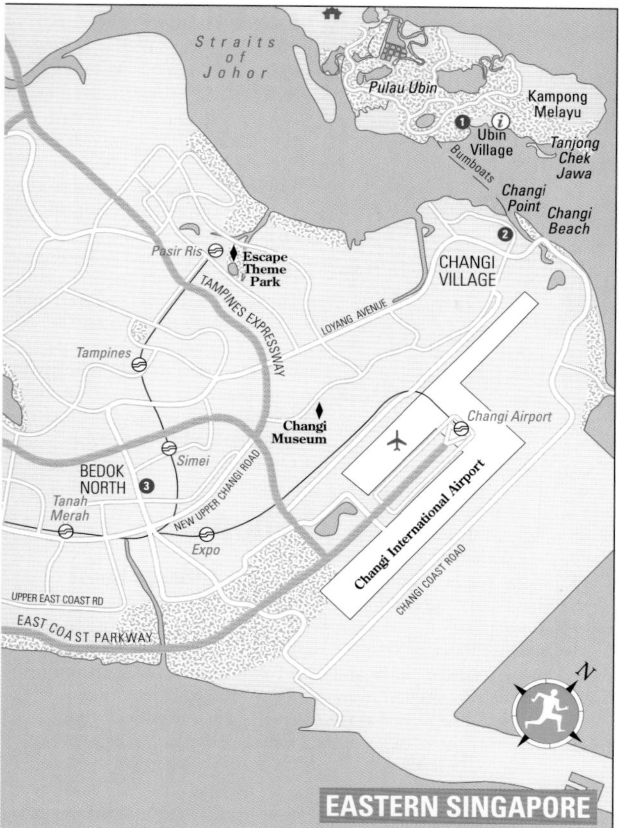




with a network of dirt tracks, making it ideal for exploring by mountain bike.

On arrival off the boat in Ubin Village, swing by the information kiosk (daily 8.30am–5pm; ⓣ65424108, ⓦwww.nparks.gov.sg) to the right of the pier to pick up an island map. A cluster of bike rental shops operates along the jetty road, charging $4–8 for a day, depending upon the bike – rates double during the school holidays. As you go, look out for monitor lizards, long-tailed macaques, lizards, kites and eagles.

In the west of the island, down a right turn marked Jalan Wat Siam, is a Thai Buddhist temple fronted by two polished wooden elephants, and complete with portraits of the king and queen of Thailand and a bookcase full of Thai books. Pictures telling the story of the life of Buddha ring the walls of the temple, along with images of various Buddhist hells.

Eastern Ubin is defined by prawn and fish farms, rubber trees and raised kampung houses. Towards Kampong

▲ BUDDHIST MONK AT BUDDHIST TEMPLE, UBIN

Melayu, in the southeast, are some beautifully maintained and brightly painted examples of kampung-style stilt houses. Beyond the village, Tanjong Chek Jawa at the far eastern tip of the island constitutes Ubin's most pristine patch of mangrove, and offers the chance to see mudskippers, crabs, seabirds and other wildlife; free guided tours can be arranged in advance at the island's information kiosk.

### Escape Theme Park

1 Pasir Ris Close ⓣ65819112, ⓦwww.escapethemepark.com.sg. Mon & Wed–Fri 4–10pm, Sat & Sun 10am–10pm. Adults $16, kids $8, including all rides (one go-cart ride). Bus #354 from Pasir Ris MRT. If you have kids in tow, you'll be glad of the Escape Theme Park – Singapore's largest – which boasts fifteen fairground-style rides, among them the Cadbury Inverter, the Daytona Multi-tier Go Kart and Asia's highest flume ride, Wet & Wild. Clowns wander the park's byways, offering light relief while you queue for rides, and in the central pavilion there are oodles of games, galleries and food outlets.

## Shops

### Katong Antiques House

208 East Coast Rd ⓣ63458544. Katong Antiques House is a dark, cluttered Aladdin's cave of Asian collectables, including Peranakan artefacts, amassed by owner Peter Wee; through its swing doors are tiffin carriers,

▼ CYCLING ON PULAU UBIN

Peranakan furniture, slippers and wedding costumes, and Chinese porcelain. To visit, you'll need to call ahead to book an appointment.

### Rumah Bebe

113 East Coast Rd. A delightful Peranakan shop, Rumah Bebe sells beaded shoes and handbags, costume jewellery, porcelain tiffin carriers and the traditional garb – *kebaya* and sarong – of Nonya women.

## Eating

### Chilli Padi

11 Joo Chiat Place ☎62751002. Red batik ceiling drapes and tablecloths bring homely warmth to this moderately-priced, family-run restaurant, whose Nonya dishes, like spicy chilli fish and *popiah* (spring rolls), have justly won it plaudits galore. The jars of *kaya* and curry pastes on sale make unusual gifts to take home.

▲ EAST COAST SEAFOOD CENTRE

### East Coast Seafood Centre

East Coast Park. Whichever operation you choose at this seafront complex of restaurants you choose to dine at, you're sure of a tremendous meal. This is the place to try messy, marvellous chilli crab – a contender for Singapore's national dish. Expect to pay $60–80 for a finger-licking feast for two.

### Guan Hoe Soon

214 Joo Chiat Rd ☎63442761. Mon & Wed–Sun 9am–9.30pm. Now over fifty years old, *Guan Hoe Soon* has been turning out fine Nonya cuisine for over fifty years. To round off your meal try the refreshing *chen dool* (coconut milk, red beans, sugar, green jelly and ice). A meal will cost around $40 for two, with beer.

### Katong laksa stalls

Junction of East Coast and Ceylon roads, Katong. Singaporeans travel from far and wide to taste the peerless Katong *laksa* served up from this venerable clutch of stalls. Tourists yet to master the art of eating with chopsticks will appreciate the fact that the noodles here are chopped fine enough to be eaten with a spoon.

### Mum's Kitchen

02-06, 3015 Bedok North St 5, Bedok ☎63460969. Daily 11am–10pm. At *Mum's*, in the sleepy suburb of Bedok, the emphasis is on home-cooked food, Nonya-based, though with other Asian incursions. House speciality Mum's Curry is wonderful, and best chased down by homemade barley water; special business lunches (Mon–Fri) offer three courses at $18 for two.

### Pasta Fresca Seasports Centre

1210 East Coast Parkway ☎64418140. Daily 11.30am–midnight. There are peerless views out to sea from this *atap* hut located within a sailing club just above the beach; the reasonably priced pizzas, pastas, meat and fish dishes are not at all bad, either. At night the lights of the tankers docked south of Singapore look like fairy lights strung along the horizon.

### Peranakan Inn

210 East Coast Rd ☎64406195. Daily 11am–3pm & 6–10.30pm. As much effort goes into the food as went into the renovation of this immaculate, bright-green shophouse restaurant, which offers authentic Nonya favourites at around $10 a dish. Try the *babi chin* (stewed pork flavoured with *miso*).

### Sin Lam Huat

Ubin Village, Ubin Island. Daily noon–7pm. *Sin Lam Huat* may be a spit-and-sawdust operation with basic plastic tables and chairs, but its specialities of chilli crab and fried chicken are simply the tastiest grub on Ubin.

### Tekong Seafood

01-2100 Blk 6, Changi Village Rd ☎65428923. *Tekong* offers high-quality but moderately priced Cantonese/Teochew seafood dishes – the steamed fish with sour prunes is particularly fab – in an open-fronted dining area. The restaurant is just a five-minute stroll from Changi Point jetty, so is best visited before or after a trip to Ubin.

# Western Singapore

**Western Singapore is the state's manufacturing heart, but much of the region remains remarkably verdant. From Mount Faber, a modest mound 3km west of Chinatown that commands panoramic views over the city and Sentosa to the south, a string of attractions threads west across the island. The battle for Singapore during World War II is remembered at Reflections at Bukit Chandu, while Chinese history and legend are celebrated at the fabulously garish Haw Par Villa. North of here, expat-oriented Holland Village offers the best eating and shopping in the region, though if you have children in tow, you'll want to push on further to Jurong Lake, site of the imaginative Singapore Science Centre. Undoubtedly the pick of the western sights for kids and adults alike is Jurong BirdPark, 3km southwest of the lake, which is home to an astonishing range of feathered creatures. All of Western Singapore's attractions are easily accessible from the city by bus and MRT.**

### Mount Faber

Cable car runs daily 8.30am–9pm; $10.90 return, children $5.50; $15, children $8 for glass cabin; prices cover round-trip taking in Mount Faber and Sentosa. HarbourFront MRT. More a hillock than a mountain, Mount Faber may only be 106 metres high but it commands fine views of Singapore, Keppel Harbour, Sentosa and beyond. Originally called Telok Blangah, the mount was once the seat of Singapore's *temenggong*, or chieftain; it was awarded its current name in 1845, after government engineer, Captain Charles Edward Faber. The summit can be accessed by road, but it's more fun to take one of the cable cars that rock across the skyline and up from the HarbourFront shopping centre-cum-marine terminal before looping back down and across to Sentosa. There's a strong souvenir shop presence around the cable car station, but if you head on into Mount Faber Park you'll be rewarded with palms, bougainvillea and rhododendrons, and bars and dining areas that sport panoramic views.

### Reflections at Bukit Chandu

31K Pepys Rd, Pasir Panjang ⓣ63327978, ⓦwww.s1942.org.sg. Tues–Sun 9am–5pm. $2. Bus #10, #30, #143 or #188 from HarbourFront MRT. The defence of the district of Pasir Panjang against the Japanese in 1942 by the 1st and 2nd Battalions of the Malay Regiment is remembered at Reflections at Bukit Chandu, a low-key World War II interpretive centre 3km west of Mount Faber. Facing some 13,000 advancing Japanese soldiers, the battalions chose to fight to the death rather than retreat, and Reflections uses exhibits and photographs to tell the soldiers' story, and to track their unsuccessful defence of

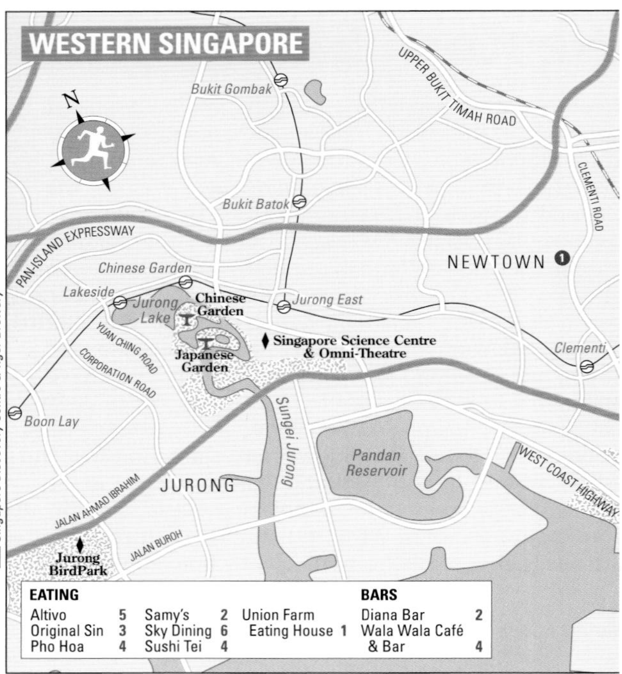


Malaya. Visitors experience the sounds of battle, and can feel at first hand the cold weight of a cast-iron helmet and a rifle, and the fear and claustrophobia of watch duty in a pillbox. However, this is no celebration of war. Rather, the emphasis is upon sombre contemplation, with features such as the Well of Reflection and the Windows of Memories encouraging visitors to ponder the purpose of war and to muse over the terrible loss of life that occurred in this part of Singapore.

## Haw Par Villa

262 Pasir Panjang Rd. Daily 9am–7pm. Free. Bus #200 from Buona Vista MRT, #143 from HarbourFront or #51 from Chinatown. As an entertaining exercise in bad taste, Haw Par Villa has few equals. Located 7km west of the downtown area, it's a gaudy, gory parade of over a thousand grotesque statues of characters and creatures from Chinese legend and religion. Fu Lu Shou, Confucius and the Laughing Buddha all put in an appearance, as does a fantastical menagerie of snakes, dragons, elephants, kissing locusts, monkeys and crabs with women's heads. The best – and most gruesome – statues are in the Ten Courts of Hell exhibit (daily 9am–5pm; $2), which depicts sinners undergoing a ghastly range of tortures meted out by hideous demons. Prostitutes are shown drowned in pools of blood, drug addicts tied to a red-hot copper pillar, thieves and gamblers frozen into blocks of ice

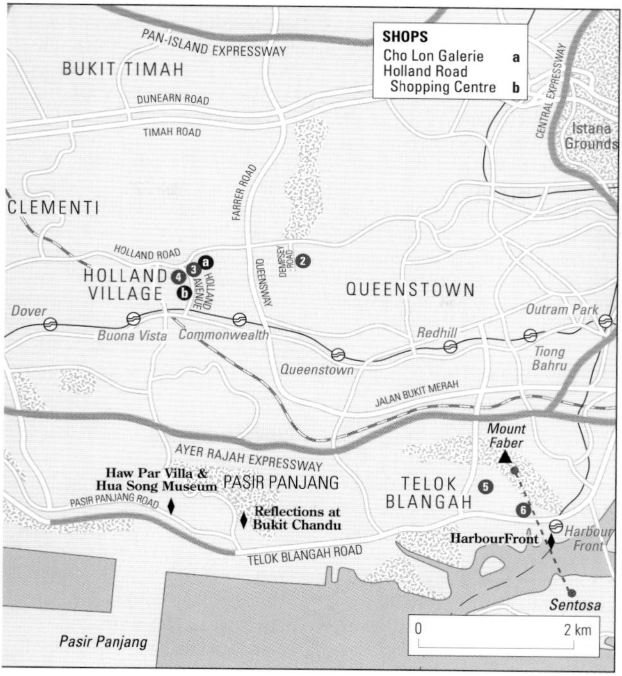

▲ TEN COURTS OF HELL, HAW PAR VILLA

and moneylenders who charge exorbitant interest rates thrown onto a hill of knives. Elsewhere, another series of statues retells the classic Chinese legend of the monk Xuanzang's journey into the West in search of Buddhist scriptures. The trials and tribulations that beset the monk and his disciples, featuring such characters as the Spider Women, the Monkey God and the Scarlet Child, are all colourfully depicted.

### Hua Song Museum

Haw Par Villa Ⓦ www.huasong.org. Tues–Sun noon–7pm. $8.40. A new attraction, the Hua Song Museum has taken up residence on the western flank of Haw Par Villa. It uses story boards, life-sized characters and tableaux to trace the struggles of Chinese emigrants from the early nineteenth century onwards, as they settled, assimilated and flourished around the world. In the Floating Hell gallery, a model of the cramped sleeping quarters on board a Chinese junk conveys the hardships migrants endured as they journeyed to their new lives, and the struggles they faced to stay alive once ashore. From there, the museum tells of how they adjusted to life in their adopted lands while still, with the support of their clan associations, preserving their ancestral identities. Food, one of the cornerstones of Chinese culture, merits its own gallery, where visitors become acquainted with the cooking implements and ingredients of its cuisine, with the help of a replica model of a traditional Chinese kitchen.

### Holland Village

Holland Village is a short walk from Buona Vista MRT station, or bus #7 from Orchard Boulevard also stops here. Named after colonial architect Hugh Holland, Holland Village has long been a stronghold of monied expats, and the resultant shops and restaurants make it a pleasing place to browse, drink and dine. Off Lorong Liput, alongside the Holland Road Shopping Centre,

▼ SINGAPORE SCIENCE CENTRE

▲ CHINESE GARDEN

is Lorong Mambong, which is home to a thriving restaurant scene and craft shops specializing in ceramic elephants, dragon pots, porcelain, rattan and bamboo products. Pasar Holland, opposite the shops, is a small, tumbledown market selling fruit, flowers, fish and meat, as well as housing a handful of hawker stalls.

## Singapore Science Centre and Omni-Theatre

Singapore Science Centre ⓣ64252500, ⓦwww.science.edu.sg; Tues–Sun 10am–6pm; $6, children $3. Omni-Theatre call ⓣ64252500 for details of current movie or check the website or local press; times vary; $10, kids $5. Jurong East MRT station, then bus #335, or brave the ten-minute walk. At the Singapore Science Centre, southeast of Jurong Lake, one thousand hands-on exhibits are designed to inject interest into even the most impenetrable scientific principles. Most visitors are local schoolchildren, who sweep around in vast, deafening waves. Exhibitions focus on such diverse disciplines as space science, aviation, genetics, marine ecology and IT, and give you the chance to experience sight through an insect's eyes, write in Braille, speak with a frog's voice and see a thermal heat reflection of yourself.

Within the Science Centre's grounds, the Omni-Theatre features heart-stopping movies about science, space, history and adventure sports shown, planetarium-style, on a huge dome screen. Recently, it has also started showing blockbusters like *Harry Potter* and *Lord of the Rings*.

## The Chinese and Japanese Gardens

Jurong Lake. Daily 6am–11pm. Free. The pagodas, carp ponds, pavilions, bridges, arches and weeping willows of the Chinese and Japanese gardens provide an attractive setting for a relaxing afternoon. The Bonzai Garden (daily 9am–5pm; free), within the garden complex, is particularly worth a browse for its hundreds of miniature trees on raised plinths. To see the gardens at their busiest, come on the day of the annual Moon Cake Festival, when they stay open late so that children can parade with their lanterns after dark.

▲ AUSTRALIAN RAINBOW LORIKEET AT JURONG BIRDPARK

### Jurong BirdPark

Jalan Ahmad Ibrahim, Jurong ⓣ62650022, ⓦwww.birdpark.com.sg. Daily 9am–6pm; $14, children $7. Boon Lay MRT station, then bus #194 or #251. One of Singapore's finest attractions, a trip to the Jurong BirdPark could occupy you for most of the day. The park contains nine thousand birds from over six hundred species, making it the biggest bird collection in Southeast Asia. A ride on the Panorail (9am–5pm; $4, children $2), which loops around and above the entire extent of the park, is a good way to get your bearings. Be sure to catch the Waterfall Aviary, where visitors can walk amongst 1500 free-flying birds in a specially created tropical rainforest, dominated by a thirty-metre-high waterfall. Other exhibits to seek out are: the colourful Australian Lory Loft; the Southeast Asian Birds, where a tropical thunderstorm is simulated daily at noon; the Penguin Parade (feeding times 10.30am & 3.30pm); and the World of Darkness, which swaps day for night with the aid of a system of reversed lighting, so that its nocturnal residents don't snooze throughout the park's opening hours. Free bird shows are put on throughout the day, the best of which is "Kings of the Skies" (4pm) – a *tour de force* of speed-flying by trained eagles, hawks and falcons; other shows worth catching are "World of Hawks" (10am) and the "All Star Bird Show" (11am & 3pm). Snacks and drinks are on sale at the complex entrance.

### The Singapore Discovery Centre

510 Upper Jurong Rd, Jurong ⓣ67926188, ⓦwww.sdc.com.sg. Tues–Fri 9am–7pm. $9, children $5. Boon Lay MRT station and then bus #193. The emphasis of the hands-on Singapore Discovery Centre is mainly on Singapore's history, technological achievements and national defences, making it a popular outing for local school groups, but there are exhibits with broader appeal. Motion simulator rides let you experience flying a jet or driving a tank, for example, and there's a clutch of virtual reality games. In the grounds outside the centre are a cluster of military vehicles of varying vintages, and an imaginative playground complete with its own maze.

### Tiger Brewery

459 Jalan Ahmad Ibrahim ⓣ68603007, ⓦwww.tigerbeer.com. Tours Mon–Fri 9.30am, 11am, 2.30pm & 5.30pm; free; minimum 10 people, though if you're on your own it's worth phoning ahead to ask if you can tag along with a pre-arranged group. Boon Lay MRT, then bus #192. Twenty-two kilometres west of the Padang is the home of one of Singapore's best-loved exports, Tiger Beer. The flagship brew of the Asia Pacific Breweries Limited has been brewed in Singapore since 1931, and today the tiger beneath a palm tree that adorns the label on every bottle can be seen in ads across the state. A tour of the brewery begins with a film detailing its history, after which you walk through its space-age brewing, bottling and canning halls. You conclude with a sample of Tiger's various brews in the site's own bar.

▲ THE FIRST EVER BOTTLE OF TIGER BEER

## Shops

### Cho Lon Galerie

43 Jalan Merah Saga, Holland Village. Named after the Chinatown district of Ho Chi Minh City, Cho Lon specializes in Chinese and Vietnamese furniture and crafts. If you fall for a sizeable item, don't worry – staff can arrange for transportation to your home country.

### Holland Road Shopping Centre

211 Holland Ave. The place to head for if you want to purchase Asian art, crafts or textiles, with shops on two levels where you can buy anything from an Indian pram to a Chinese opium pipe. For furniture and housewares with a Balinese accent, try Lim's Arts & Living.

▲ LIM'S ARTS AND LIVING

▲ ALFRESCO DINING IN HOLLAND VILLAGE

# Eating

### Altivo

109 Mount Faber Rd ☎63779688. Restaurant open daily noon–10.30pm; bar open daily 9pm–3am. Singapore favourites (*kway teow*, *laksa*, chicken rice) are all well executed at this breezy restaurant, though the menu also embraces north African and European influences – good news if you can't face another bowl of noodles. Outside, *Altivo*'s bar offers starlit cocktail-supping overlooking the twinkling lights of Singapore harbour. Decor – earthenware jars and creepers – is understated, allowing the view to speak for itself.

### Original Sin

01-62 Blk 43, Jalan Merah Saga, Holland Village ☎64755605. Tues–Sun noon–3pm & 6–10.30pm. *Original Sin* offers quality if pricey vegetarian Mediterranean fare in a rust-and-aquamarine-painted dining room. The *meze* plate makes an enticing appetizer, after which you could do worse than opt for pizza Ibizi (topped with roasted pumpkin, avocado, Spanish onion, asparagus and cheese). It also has one of the most extensive wine lists in Singapore.

### Pho Hoa

18 Lorong Mambong, Holland Village. Daily 11am–10pm. Part of a global noodle franchise, *Pho Hoa* knocks out decent and cheap *pho*, or Vietnamese rice noodle soup, as well as rice plates such as *com suon* (grilled pork chop, rice and salad). The menu explains the fundamentals of *pho*, and you can sample a beginner's version, create your own, or try the Adventurer's choice, with steak, meatballs, tripe and brisket.

### Samy's

Singapore Civil Service Club, Block 25 Dempsey Rd, Holland Village

☎64745618. Bus #7 from Orchard MRT; alight when you see Pierce Rd to the left. Once you've sunk a few Tigers at *Diana Bar* next door (see below), you'll be ready for a *Samy's* curry, served on a banana leaf, and best enjoyed, not in the spit-and-sawdust dining area, but at a table overlooking the trees on the fairy-lit verandah. Two pay around $15, and beers can be ordered from the club.

### Sky Dining

Mount Faber ☎63779688, Ⓔskydining@mountfaber.com.sg. Daily 6.30–8.30pm. Cars carry maximum of four adults plus one child. One of Singapore's quirkier dining experiences has you eating onboard a cable car looping 70m above sea level between Mount Faber and Sentosa. Prices for the largely Western set menus range from $88 to $158 for two. A children's menu comes in at $20.

### Sushi Tei

20 Lorong Mambong, Holland Village. Daily 11.30am–10pm. A popular chain, this is a cross-fertilization of a Tokyo sushi bar and an airport baggage reclaim: diners snatch sushi ($2–8) from the conveyor belt looping the bar.

### Union Farm Eating House

435a Clementi Rd, Clementi ☎64662776. Bus #154 from Clementi MRT and alight at Maju army camp. Daily 11.30am–8.30pm. The *Union Farm Eating House* is located in a former poultry farm, and the palms and bamboos that surround it ensure it retains a rural feel. The Chinese food on offer is great, but most wonderful – and messy – is the house special, *chee pow kai* (marinated chicken wrapped in greaseproof paper and deep fried). $15 buys enough for two.

## Bars

### Diana Bar

Singapore Civil Service Club, Blk 25 Dempsey Rd, Holland Village. Daily 10.30am–10.30pm. There's something of the officers' mess about this quaint bar, located in an ex-army barracks on the road to Holland Village. High ceilings, clapboard walls and bamboo chairs make it a welcome change from the Buddhas, neon and black leather that define most Singaporean bars. Should the hunger pangs strike, there's a Chinese menu on hand – and *Samy's* (see opposite) is just next door.

### Wala Wala Café & Bar

31 Lorong Mambong, Holland Village ☎64624288. Sun–Thurs 4pm–1am, Fri & Sat 4pm–2am. This rocking Holland Village joint, now into its second decade, serves Boddingtons, Stella and Hoegaarden and features a generous happy hour (4–9pm). A live band plays upstairs in the *Bar Above*, while the ground floor's flatscreen TVs will appeal to sports fans.

# Sentosa

**Tiny Sentosa is the most developed of the many little islands that stud the waters immediately south of Singapore (lending the island's name, which means "tranquillity" in Malay, a certain irony). Heavily promoted for its attractions, beaches, sports facilities and hotels – and successfully so, as five million visitors descend upon it every year – it's a contrived but enjoyable experience, easily accessible from the mainland by a five-hundred-metre causeway and a necklace of cable cars. Sentosa boasts three attractions that outshine all others – Underwater World, a riot of aquatic life and colour; Images of Singapore, where dioramas bring the story of the state to life; and historic Fort Siloso – but there are a host of B-list sights on hand to fill in idle hours. Measuring 3km by 1km, Sentosa is too large to be easily walkable; buses or rented bikes provide a more practical means of touring its sights.**

## Underwater World

Daily 9am–9pm. $19.50, kids $12.50; includes access to Dolphin Lagoon.

At the Underwater World, a moving walkway carries you along a 100-metre acrylic tunnel that snakes through two large tanks. Sharks lurk menacingly

## Visiting Sentosa

### Transport

The new **Sentosa Express** light rail system is due to go live in early 2007, and will link the island to HarbourFront MRT. Until then, you'll need to take either a **bus** ($2; follow signs from HarbourFront and look out for the orange Sentosa Bus) or a **cable car** to the island (daily 8.30am–9pm; return trip $10.90, children $5.50; glass-bottomed cabin $15, children $8). Once on Sentosa, the least exerting way of getting around is to hop on the free buses (there are four colour-coded lines) that ply its roads. A fifth service, the **Beach Train**, shuttles along the island's south coast. Alternatively, **bikes** can be rented from beside the ferry terminal for $2–5 an hour.

### Admission

A $2 charge for admission to Sentosa is levied when you arrive on the island, either at the Visitor Arrival Centre at the foot of the causeway linking Sentosa to the mainland, or at the Cable Car Aerial Plaza. Admission to several lesser sights is included in this, though visiting more popular attractions engenders a further charge.

### Information

For up-to-date tourist information on Sentosa, call ⓣ67368672 or check ⓦwww.sentosa.com.sg.

▲ CABLE CAR VIEW OF THE CITY

on all sides, huge stingrays drape themselves languidly above you, and immense shoals of gaily coloured fish dart to and fro. The sensation of being engulfed by sea life – there are more than 2500 fish from some 250 species here – is breathtaking, and the nearest you'll get to the ocean floor without a wet suit. If that isn't enough to get the adrenaline pumping, there's even the chance to dive with the sharks by pre-arrangement (call ⓣ62750030 for more details; $95 per person). The foyer is home to various crabs, including the gruesome coconut crab, and a touch pool beside the entrance allows you to pick up starfish and sea cucumbers. Beyond that is the Marine Theatre, which screens educational films throughout the day.

### Dolphin Lagoon

Palawan Beach. Daily 10.30am–6pm (Meet the Dolphin shows Mon–Fri 11am, 1.30pm, 3.30pm & 5.30pm). Free admission with Underwater World ticket. The marine acrobatics of the Dolphin Lagoon's resident

▲ UNDERWATER WORLD

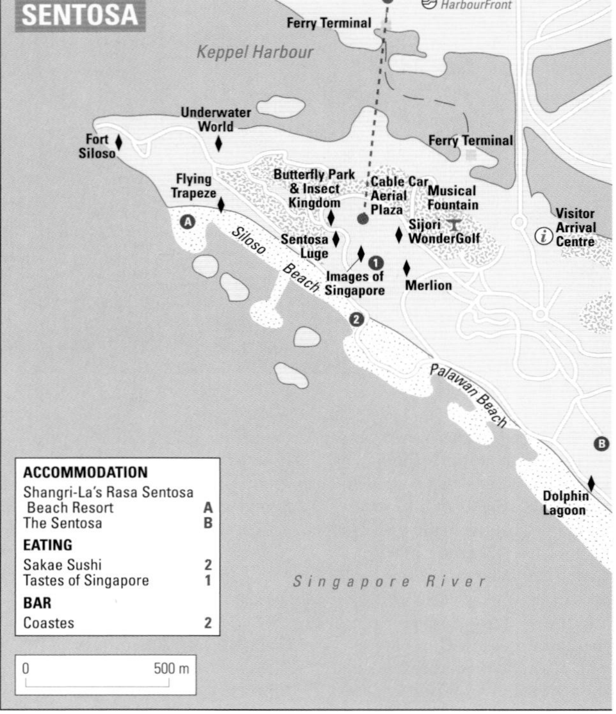


school of highly intelligent Indo-Pacific humpback dolphins are best viewed during one of its regular Meet the Dolphins sessions, when these delightful creatures demonstrate their prowess at tail-walking and other tricks. Visitors sometimes get the chance to wade with the dolphins, and perhaps even receive a peck on the cheek from one of them. If wading sounds too pedestrian for you, $120 will buy the opportunity to swim with dolphins (maximum nine people at once).

### Images of Singapore

Daily 9am–9pm. $10, kids $7. At Images of Singapore, life-sized dioramas present the history and heritage of Singapore from its early days as a fourteenth-century trading post through to the surrender of the Japanese in 1945. Though the scene-setting audiovisual presentation is contrived and flaky, and some of the wax dummies look as if they've been pinched from clothes shop windows, the effect is nonetheless fascinating. Iconic images from Singapore's past – Raffles forging a treaty with the island's Malay rulers; rubber tappers at the Botanical Gardens; coolies working the Singapore River; the street barber, satay man and dhoby at work – spring to life, and there

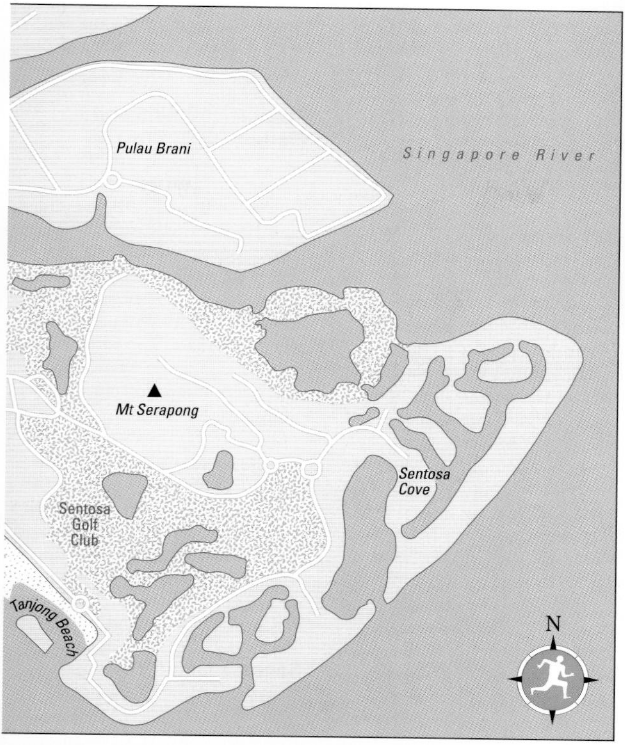

Pulau Brani

Singapore River

Mt Serapong

Sentosa Cove

Sentosa Golf Club

Tanjong Beach

N

▲ DIORAMA AT IMAGES OF SINGAPORE

are actors dressed as coolies and kampung dwellers on hand to provide further insight. There are more wax dummies in the Singapore Celebrates area, this time dolled up in festive costumes to represent Singapore's various ethnic celebrations.

## Fort Siloso

Daily 10am–6pm. $8, children $5. A trip up to Fort Siloso, at the far western tip of the island, forms another of Sentosa's highlights. The fort – actually a cluster of buildings and gun emplacements above a series of tunnels bored into the island – guarded Singapore's western approaches from the 1880s until 1956, but was rendered obsolete in 1942, when the Japanese moved down into Singapore from Malaysia. Today, the recorded voice of Battery Sergeant Major (BSM) Cooper talks you through a mock-up of a nineteenth-century barracks, complete with living quarters, guard room, laundry and assault course. Be sure to check out the Surrender Chambers, recently moved from Images of Singapore, where life-sized figures re-enact the British and Japanese surrenders of 1942 and 1945, respectively. After that you can explore the complex's hefty gun emplacements and tunnels.

## Musical Fountain and Merlion

Shows at 5pm, 5.30pm, 7.40pm & 8.40pm. Merlion 10am–8pm; $8, children $5. By the early evening, many of Sentosa's attractions are closed, but not so the Musical Fountain, which is either cute or tacky, depending on your point of view. The fountain dances along to a throbbing soundtrack, with lights, lasers, CGI cartoon characters and pyrotechnics adding to the effect.

Overlooking the display is the Merlion, a 37-metre-high statue of Singapore's tourism totem that takes centre stage in the shows. It's possible to walk up to the viewing decks at the top of the Merlion from where there are great views of Singapore's harbour, skyline and surrounding islands.

## Sentosa Luge

Mon–Thurs 10am–6pm, Fri–Sun 10am–7pm. One ride $8. One of the island's newest attractions, the Sentosa luge is an enjoyable carting track that is sure to unlock the hidden child within you. Vehicles are a cross between

▲ FORT SILOSO

go-carts and toboggans, and have a sound braking mechanism, meaning your kids aren't going to come to any harm. After you've reached the end of the ride, a chairlift will take you back up to the starting line.

### Sijori WonderGolf

Daily 9am–7pm. $8, children $4. Golfing purists may scoff at the imaginatively themed miniature holes here, but negotiating the traps, tunnels, slopes and other obstacles is actually lots of fun. There are three eighteen-hole courses to play, so you could easily spend a good few hours at WonderGolf.

### Butterfly Park and Insect Kingdom

Daily 9am–6.30pm. $10, children $6. Stuffed with all sorts of creepy-crawlies, this attraction should appeal greatly to children. The grounds are home to thousands of butterflies from some fifty species; within the Insect Kingdom, meanwhile, are enough beetles, bugs, spiders and scorpions to give more squeamish visitors nightmares for months.

### Sentosa's Beaches

Probably the best option on Sentosa, after a visit to one or two attractions, is to head for one of the three beaches – Siloso, Palawan and Tanjong – on the island's western coast. Created with thousands of cubic metres of imported white sand and scores of coconut palms, they offer canoes, surfboards and aqua-bikes for rent, as well as plain old deck chairs. The water here is great for swimming and Singapore does not demand the same modesty on its beaches as Malaysia, although topless and nude bathing are out. From Palawan Beach, a suspended rope bridge connects Sentosa with a tiny islet that's the southernmost part of continental Asia, while in recent years, Singapore's annual Dragon Boat Festival has been held off Siloso Beach. There are also beach raves, Singapore-style, from time to time, which are advertised well in advance in the local press.

## Eating

### Sakae Sushi

Siloso Beach. Mon–Thurs 11am–9.30pm, Fri & Sat 11am–11pm, Sun 10am–9.30pm. Said to boast the longest sushi conveyor belt in Asia, the Sentosa branch of this popular chain is well equipped to serve the vast range of sushi, sashimi, *ramen*, *teriyaki*, *dinburi*, *tempura* and *teppanyaki* on its menu.

▲ SILOSO BEACH

### Tastes of Singapore

Imbiah Lookout. Daily 10am–9pm. *Tastes of Singapore* has rounded up many of Singapore's defining dishes and culinary influences – Nyonya lobster *laksa*, satay chicken, and tandoori chicken among them – making it a one stop shop for diners wishing to experience a range of local flavours.

## Bars

### Coastes

Siloso Beach. Mon–Thur 11am–11pm, Fri 11am–1am, Sat 9am–1am, Sun 9am–11pm. By day *Coastes* is a chilled, beachfront bar with chunky *Robinson Crusoe* furniture, comfy sun beds and double hammocks, all shaded by tall palm trees. After sunset (which can be fabulous), the music pumps up, Ibiza party-style. Cold beers, cocktails and snacks are available, day and night.

# Accommodation

# Accommodation

Finding a room in Singapore needn't be too pricey; there are good deals available if your expectations aren't too lofty or – at the budget end of the scale – you don't mind sharing a dorm. Advance booking generally isn't really necessary unless your visit coincides with Chinese New Year or Hari Raya – though booking ahead could secure you a more advantageous room rate.

Orchard Road boasts Singapore's greatest concentration of mid- to upper-bracket hotels; stay here and you'll have some of Singapore's best shopping on the doorstep and be well placed to explore the rest of the city. East of Orchard Road, the Colonial District offers a broader range of options, from the dormitories and plain partitioned rooms of its crash pads, to its classy five-star hotels – among them Singapore's defining accommodation option, venerable *Raffles Hotel*. Chinatown has in recent years developed a delightful cluster of boutique hotels combining Chinoiserie and antique furniture and fittings to create an air of Oriental nostalgia, while Little India has moulded itself as a backpacker enclave, with a number of cheery budget options putting the tired addresses on Beach Road and Bencoolen Street to shame. Alternatively, staying on Sentosa Island sets you close to beaches and tourist attractions, but away from the bustle of the city.

The cheapest beds are in the communal dormitories of the island's backpacker addresses – variously called hostels, rest-houses, homestays or guesthouses – where you'll pay $10 or less a night. These proliferate in the Colonial District, Little India and Chinatown. These options usually have private rooms at the $20–30 mark, but they are likely to be tiny, bare, divided by paper-thin partitions, and offer only shared toilets and cold showers. Paying another $10–20 secures a bigger, a/c room, often including TV, laundry and cooking facilities, lockers and breakfast. In mid-range hotels, a room for two with a/c, private bathroom and TV will set you back around $60–90 a night. From there, prices rise steadily; at the top end of the scale Singapore boasts some extraordinarily opulent hotels, ranging from the awesome spectacle of *Swissôtel The Stamford* – until recently the world's tallest hotel – to stylish boutique hotels such as *The Scarlet*.

## Booking accommodation

The **Singapore Hotel Association** has a booking counter at each of Changi airport's two terminals (Terminal One Mon–Thurs, Sat & Sun 7am–6am, Fri 7am–11.30pm, ⓣ65426966; Terminal Two Tues–Sun 7am–3am, Mon 7am–11.30pm, ⓣ65459789; ⓦwww.sha.org.sg) and will find you a room in the city for a $10 deposit that's deducted from your bill at the end of your stay. Touts at the airport also hand out flyers advertising rooms in guesthouses and hostels. If you prefer to plan ahead, you might wish to book online through ⓦwww.stayinsingapore.com, ⓦwww.singaporehotelbooking.com or ⓦwww.ehotelsingapore.com.

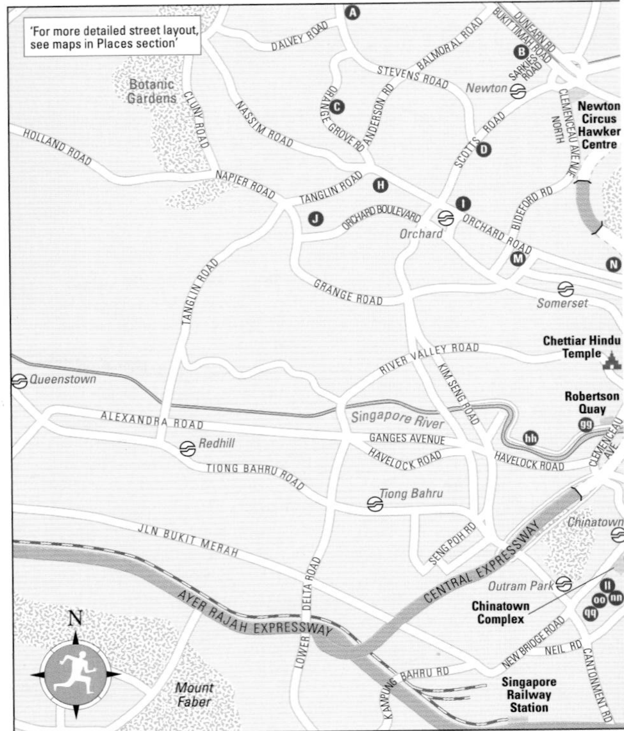


| | | | | | |
|---|---|---|---|---|---|
| Hotel 1929 | nn | Damenlou Hotel | mm | The Inn at Temple Street | kk |
| Ah Chew Hotel | S | Dickson Court | F | InnCrowd Hostel I | E |
| Albert Court Hotel | K | Fullerton Hotel | jj | Intercontinental | R |
| Aliwal Park Hotel | L | Gallery Hotel | hh | Lee Boarding House | V |
| Beach Hotel | W | Goodwood Park Hotel | D | Lee Traveller's Club | Z |
| City Bayview | X | Hawaii Hostel | P | Marina Mandarin Hotel | ee |
| Conrad Centennial Singapore | dd | Hilton Singapore | H | Meritus Mandarin Hotel | M |
| | | | | Metropole Hotel | aa |

## Around the Padang

**Swissôtel The Stamford 2 Stamford Rd ⓣ63388585, ⓦwww.singapore-stamford.swissotel.com.** The views are as splendid as you'd expect from the second-tallest hotel in the world, though the upper-floor rooms aren't for those with vertigo. There are 1253 classy rooms here, all with high-speed Internet access, cable TV and in-house movies. There are oodles of restaurants and bars on site, plus the Raffles Amrita Spa – Asia's largest – and an MRT station downstairs. $300.

## Raffles Hotel and the northern Colonial District

**Ah Chew Hotel 496 North Bridge Rd ⓣ68370356.** The common areas have "Wild West" swing doors at this Chinese

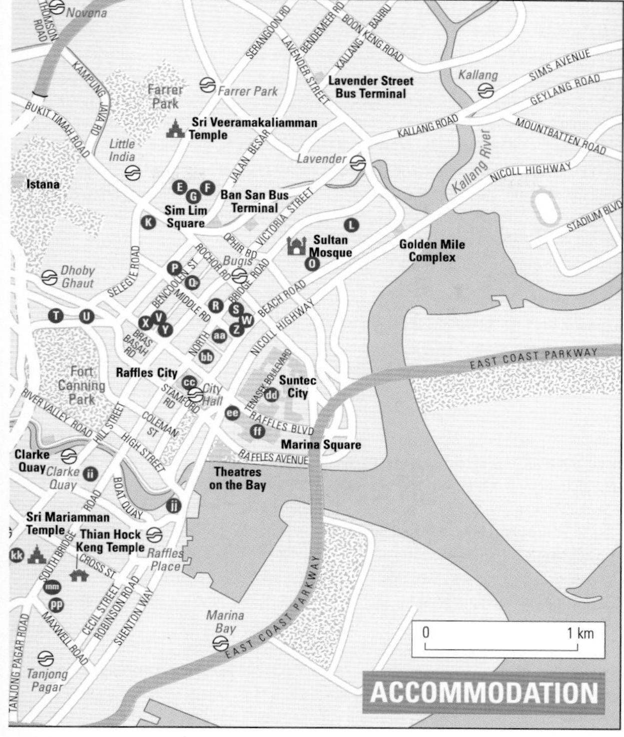


| | | | | | |
|---|---|---|---|---|---|
| Metropolitan Y | A | Royal Peacock Hotel | ll | Hotel Supreme | N |
| New Majestic Hotel | qq | Scarlett Hotel | pp | Swissôtel The Stamford | cc |
| New Sandy's Place | B | Shangri-La Hotel | C | Summer Tavern | ii |
| Oriental Singapore | ff | Singapore Marriott Hotel | I | A Traveller's Rest-Stop | oo |
| Perak Lodge | G | Sleepy Sam's | O | Waterloo Hostel | Y |
| Raffles Hotel | bb | South East Asia Hotel | Q | YMCA International House | U |
| Regent Singapore | J | | | YWCA Fort Canning Lodge | T |
| Robertson Quay Hotel | gg | | | | |

hotel that's crammed with period furniture, and run by T-shirted old men lounging on antique opium couches. Rooms are simple but charismatic and there are also fan and a/c dorms. Baggage storage and self-service laundry facilities are also available. Dorms $10–12; rooms $26.

**Beach Hotel** **95 Beach Rd ⓣ63367712, ⓦwww.beachhotel.com.sg**. Professionally run, very tidy and relatively salubrious, the *Beach Hotel* gives you a central base from which to explore. Rooms are cheaply furnished and a bit tacky, but all come with cable TV and international dialling. $90.

**City Bayview** **30 Bencoolen St ⓣ63372882, ⓦwww.citybayview.com.sg** A pleasant, recently renovated and comfortable mid-range hotel, with a compact rooftop swimming pool and a friendly, modern café. Rooms are a little small, but their light, neutral colour palette make them welcoming enough. $140.

## A guide to prices

Prices quoted are for the cheapest double room, with the exception of guest-houses with dormitories, where dorm bed prices are also listed. Single occupancy tends to cost the same or, at best, fifteen percent less than double occupancy. A light breakfast – toast, fruit, coffee or tea – is usually included in prices at the lower end of the scale; in hotels, the bill tends to be exclusive of breakfast. The majority of mid-range and upmarket hotels make no charge for children under twelve if they are occupying existing spare beds in rooms. However, if you require an extra bed to be put in your room, ten to fifteen percent of the room rate is usually charged. Cots are provided free.

Conrad Centennial Singapore **2 Temasek Blvd ⓣ63348888, ⓦsingapore.conradmeetings.com.** This relatively recent arrival has elbowed its way into the very top ranks of the island's hotels, and is very popular with business travellers. All imaginable comforts can be found within its monolithic structure, including pool, spa, fitness club and a range of food and beverage outlets. $400.

Hawaii Hostel **2nd floor, 171b Bencoolen St ⓣ63384187.** This hostel offers small, tidy enough a/c rooms with breakfast included, as well as dorm beds for $12. Rooms are $35.

Intercontinental **80 Middle Rd ⓣ63387600, ⓦwww.singapore.intercontinental.com.** Besides its tastefully appointed rooms, which have a colonial theme, the *Intercontinental* boasts a swimming pool, health club and an array of excellent restaurants. The hotel is attached to the shops and cinema of Bugis Junction shopping centre, and is close to Bugis MRT. $250.

Lee Boarding House **7th floor, Peony Mansion, 46–52 Bencoolen St ⓣ63383149.** A survivor, this is an old-style crash pad with bare but clean enough rooms, a breakfast area and laundry facilities. Dorm beds are $12, rooms $30.

Lee Traveller's Club **6th floor, Fu Yuen Building, 75 Beach Rd ⓣ63395490.** Its bright and breezy common room overlooking Middle Road sets this place a cut above many of the other backpacker addresses in the area. All rooms have a/c and laundry service is available. Dorm beds $12, rooms $22.

Marina Mandarin Hotel **6 Raffles Blvd ⓣ63383388, ⓦwww.marina-mandarin.com.sg.** The convex exterior of this top-flight hotel lends it the appearance of a billowing sail, and makes for an impressive atrium. Its cool, contemporary rooms afford great harbour views. $300.

Metropole Hotel **41 Seah St ⓣ63363611, ⓦwww.metrohotel.com.** The *Metropole* is a friendly, great-value establishment, just across the road from *Raffles Hotel* and home to the excellent *Imperial Herbal Restaurant*. Though it defines itself as a hotel for business travellers on a budget, the peach-hued rooms with quilted satin bedspreads give it a homelier feel. $115.

Oriental Singapore **5 Raffles Ave ⓣ63380066, ⓦwww.mandarinoriental.com.** The *Oriental* is one of Singapore's priciest hotels, but with very good reason. Rooms are exquisitely furnished, and all the luxuries you could want are on hand. The views out over Marina Bay and the Theatres Project are breathtaking. $320.

Raffles Hotel **1 Beach Rd ⓣ63371886, ⓦwww.raffleshotel.com.** The flagship of Singapore's tourism industry, *Raffles* takes shameless advantage of its reputation: $25 buys you a Singapore Sling and a glass to take home, while the souvenir shop stocks *Raffles* golf balls, socks and cuddly tigers. Still, it's a beautiful place, dotted with frangipani trees and palms, and the suites (there are no rooms) are as tasteful as you would expect at these prices, with Oriental carpets, louvred windows and other colonial touches. $900.

South East Asia Hotel **190 Waterloo St ⓣ63382394, ⓦwww.seahotel.com.sg.** Behind a jolly, yellow-and-white 1950s facade lie spotless doubles with a/c, TV and phone for those who appreciate a few creature comforts. Right next door is Singapore's liveliest Buddhist temple, making the place noisy but atmospheric. $77.

**Waterloo Hostel** **4th Floor, Catholic Centre Building, 55 Waterloo St ⓣ63366555, ⓦwww.waterloohostel.com.sg.** This spick-and-span Catholic-run hostel is centrally located and boasts rooms with a/c, TV and phone, as well as welcoming mixed and single-sex dorms. Complimentary breakfast is thrown in. Dorms $15–20, rooms $75.

## Fort Canning Park and the western quays

**Gallery Hotel** **76 Robertson Quay ⓣ68498686, ⓦwww.galleryhotel.com.sg.** Extravagantly lit with neon stripes at night, and boasting some striking postmodern architecture, the *Gallery* is getting listed in those trendy "hip hotel" coffee-table books. The pool is to die for, some of Singapore's coolest nightspots are on site, and all the urban-chic rooms offer free broadband access. Booking via the website may offer better rates than that listed here. $158.

**Robertson Quay Hotel** **15 Merbau Rd ⓣ67353333, ⓦwww.robertsonquayhotel.com.sg.** This cylindrical riverside hotel can't be faulted. The compact but inviting rooms off circular corridors yield great views of the river and city skyline, and there's a cute circular pool with slide and waterfall on the third-floor terrace. $120.

**YWCA Fort Canning Lodge** **6 Fort Canning Rd ⓣ63384222, ⓦwww.ywcafclodge.org.sg.** Not women-only, as you might imagine, but still a secure and friendly place with pool and tennis court – and just a stone's throw from Dhoby Ghaut MRT station. The rooms haven't seen a make-over in a while, but their bright yellow walls and cheery fabrics make them welcoming enough. $120.

## Orchard Road and around

**Goodwood Park Hotel** **22 Scotts Rd ⓣ67377411, ⓦwww.goodwoodparkhotel.com.sg.** A study in elegance, this opulent hotel may remind you of *Raffles* – both were designed by the same architect, and share a rich history. The *Goodwood Park* started life in 1900 as the Teutonia Club for German expats, only becoming a hotel in 1929, and served time as a war crimes court after World War II. The hotel's arching facades front exquisitely appointed rooms. $350.

**Hilton Singapore** **581 Orchard Rd ⓣ67372233, ⓦwww.hilton.com.** Situated in the middle of Orchard Road, this gargantuan slab of a hotel boasts every conceivable facility, from babysitting to wireless Web access, as well as five dining options. Ask for a view of Orchard Road and you can watch the shoppers moving below you like ants. $355.

**Meritus Mandarin Hotel** **333 Orchard Rd ⓣ67374411, ⓦwww.mandarin-singapore.com.** Every luxury you could hope for is available at the *Meritus Mandarin*; even if you don't stay in one of its 1200 bright, modern rooms, it's worth taking a trip up to the top-floor bar-restaurant for its magnificent view of central Singapore. $310.

**Metropolitan Y** **60 Stevens Rd ⓣ67377755, ⓦwww.mymca.org.sg.** The *Metropolitan Y* is not as central as the *YMCA* on Orchard Road, but it has perfectly adequate rooms with a/c, bathroom, TV and minibar, and is suitable for travellers in wheelchairs. $130.

**New Sandy's Place** **3c Sarkies Rd ⓣ67341431, ⓔsandygiam@hotmail.com.** The dorms and a/c single and double rooms are all very tidy in this friendly, laid-back place, set across a field from Newton MRT. Prices include a tropical fruit breakfast and a free flow of hot drinks. It's best to phone or email ahead. Dorm beds start at $13, rooms $30.

**Regent Singapore** **1 Cuscaden Rd ⓣ67338888, ⓦwww.regenthotels.com.** At the western end of Orchard Road, a short stroll from the Botanic Gardens, the *Regent* has sumptuous rooms with elegant darkwood furniture and indoor ferns, which evoke a colonial ambience. $350.

**Shangri-La Hotel** **22 Orange Grove Rd ⓣ67373644, ⓦwww.shangri-la.com.** Only five minutes from Orchard Road, this top-flight hotel has 700-plus rooms and is set in six hectares of landscaped greenery. The more contemporary rooms are in the

Valley Wing; those overlooking the free-form pool are in need of a refurb. $275.

Singapore Marriott Hotel **320 Orchard Rd ⓣ67355800, ⓦmarriott.com/property/propertypage/SINDT.** A Singaporean landmark, this superior hotel, next door to C.K. Tangs Department Store, occupies a 33-storey building with a unique pagoda-style roof. Rooms are designed in tan, fern-green and taupe with Oriental flourishes of colour, and offer fast Web access and cable TV. $330.

Hotel Supreme **15 Kramat Rd ⓣ67378333, ⓔsupremeh@starhub.net.sg.** This great-value budget hotel is well placed at the eastern end of Orchard Road. Rooms are nothing fancy, but are kept clean enough, and laundry and room service are on offer alongside many other facilities. $120.

YMCA International House **1 Orchard Rd ⓣ63366000, ⓦwww.ymcaih.com.sg.** Smack bang in the middle of town, the *YMCA* offers cheerful, unpretentious rooms, excellent sports facilities (including rooftop pool) and free room service from the *McDonald's* downstairs. Bus #36 from the airport stops right outside. Rooms $115, dorm beds $25.

## Chinatown

Hotel 1929 **50 Keong Saik Rd ⓣ62223377, ⓦwww.hotel1929.com.** This old shophouse building looks very 1929 on the outside, but the interior has been renovated to look like a twenty-first century version of the early 1960s; it's very retro chic and all tastefully done with a hip, boutique feel about it. Wacky cushions and bed covers and bright furnishings give the (smallish) rooms a funky feel. $150.

Damenlou Hotel **12 Ann Siang Rd ⓣ62211900, ⓦwww.damenlou.com.** Given its lovingly restored 1925 facade, the twelve compact but well-appointed rooms in this friendly hotel are surprisingly modern. After a pre-dinner drink on the rooftop garden overlooking Chinatown head down to the excellent *Swee Kee* restaurant. $70.

The Inn at Temple Street **36 Temple St 62215333, ⓦwww.theinn.com.sg.** Glossy and grand inside, this boutique hotel has been sculpted out of a row of Chinatown shophouses. Its owners have filled it to bursting with furnishings and curios from old Singapore. $100.

New Majestic Hotel **31–37 Bukit Pasoh Rd ⓣ65114700, ⓦwww.newmajestichotel.com.** This Chinatown classic has recently undergone major renovations, giving the interior a stylish, modern make-over that would not be out of place in New York or London. Each of its 30 rooms has been individually designed by emerging Singaporean artists, making for an eclectic feel that embraces old dentists' chairs, cast-iron bathtubs, theatre seats, hanging beds and zany murals. Rooms all have Bose stereos and plasma TVs. $140.

Royal Peacock Hotel **55 Keong Saik Rd ⓣ62233522, ⓦwww.royalpeacockhotel.com.** The silky, sassy elegance of the *Royal Peacock* won't suit all tastes, but there's no denying that its rooms (some windowless) are a bold combination of sleigh beds, gilt mirrors, bolster cushions and rich fabrics. Sculpted from ten shophouses, the hotel boasts bar, café and business services. $110.

Scarlet Hotel **33 Erskine Rd ⓣ65113333 ⓦwww.thescarlethotel.com.** Occupying a row of refurbished nineteenth-century shophouses plus an Art Deco building, the *Scarlet* is a classy boutique hotel whose common spaces are a crimson and gold extravagance of sassy fabrics, gilt mirrors and sumptuous chandeliers. On the downside, the majority of its 84 rooms are tiny, and many only have skylight windows. All, though, have free broadband access. $210.

Summer Tavern **31 Carpenter St ⓣ6535 6601, ⓦwww.summertavern.com.** This excellent a/c hostel is well located close to the Singapore River and Clarke Quay. Most of the accommodation is in dorms, though there's also the so-called "honeymoon" double room (which also has shared facilities); rates include breakfast. Free Internet access (and WiFi) is also on offer, and airport pick-ups can be arranged. Dorms $24, doubles $60.

A Traveller's Rest-Stop **5 Teck Lim St ⓣ62254812, ⓦwww.atravellersreststop.com.sg.** In a wedge-shaped building with some palpable Chinatown atmosphere, this place has clean rooms and dorms, and brightly lit corridors, and benefits from nice touches like watercolours of Old Chinatown, TVs and fridges. Dorms are $18, rooms $65.

## The CBD and Boat Quay

**Fullerton Hotel 1 Fullerton Sq, ⓣ67338388, ⓦwww.fullertonhotel.com.** Some of the chic, harmonious rooms are a touch petite, but the views on all sides of the *Fullerton* are great, whether you are facing the river, city or bay. Luxury extras include in-room Playstations, Bulgari smellies, and Internet access on the TVs – an expensive treat. See also p.97. $250.

## Little India

**Albert Court Hotel 180 Albert St ⓣ63393939, ⓦwww.albertcourt.com.sg.** This well-conceived and excellent-value boutique hotel is just a short walk from Little India and Waterloo Street. Rooms are dressed in calming neutral tones and have all the standard embellishments. $150.

**Dickson Court 3 Dickson Rd ⓣ62977811, ⓦwww.dicksoncourthotel.com.sg.** With smart, well-furnished rooms off light corridors, the peaceful *Dickson Court* is pretty good value; most corners of central Singapore are accessible from the bus stop across the road on Jalan Besar. $89.

**InnCrowd Hostel I 35 Campbell Lane ⓣ62969169, ⓦwww.the-inncrowd.com.** Singapore's best guesthouse, thanks to scrupulous cleanliness, peerless facilities and the warm welcome from its owners. Guests have free use of the kitchen and free Internet access, and lockers are available for long-term rental. If the one double room ($48) is taken you'll have to make do with a dorm bed. Dorms $18.

**Perak Lodge 12 Perak Rd ⓣ62997733, ⓦwww.peraklodge.net.** One of the new breed of upper-bracket guesthouses, set within an atmospheric blue-and-white shophouse in a back street behind the Little India arcade, and run by friendly staff. The rooms are secure (all have safes), well appointed and welcoming, and the price includes a continental breakfast. Downstairs there's an airy, residents-only living area. $115.

## Arab Quarter

**Aliwal Park Hotel 77 Aliwal St ⓣ62939022, ⓔaliwal@pacific.net.sg.** One of the few hotels in the Arab Street district, the *Aliwal* has spruce doubles with TV, a/c and attached bathrooms at competitive prices. $50.

**Sleepy Sam's 55 Bussorah St ⓣ9277 4988, ⓦwww.sleepysams.com.** Just around the corner from the Sultan Mosque, this guesthouse is welcoming and surprisingly stylish. Besides mixed and female-only dorms, it offers singles, doubles and triples, all of which share bathrooms. Breakfasts, which include plenty of exotic tropical fruit, are complimentary and served all day, and there's a kitchen for self-caterers, laundry service, and free Internet access too. Dorm beds $25, doubles $65.

## Sentosa

See Sentosa map on p.140 for hotel locations.

**The Sentosa 2 Bukit Manis Rd ⓣ62750331, ⓦwww.beaufort.com.sg.** This swanky hotel is fitted out in varnished wood, and is bounded by two eighteen-hole golf courses and a beach. Its Spa Botanica makes it the perfect place for a pampering getaway. $290.

**Shangri-La's Rasa Sentosa Beach Resort ⓣ62750100, ⓦwww.shangri-la.com.** The *Rasa Sentosa* remains the only hotel in Singapore with its own beach front and its situation on Sentosa makes it a good option if you've got kids to amuse. Adults might prefer to check out the spa or sea sports centre. Rooms with sea views cost extra but prices start at $260.

Essentials

# Arrival

Singapore's main airport is no more than a half-hour journey from the city centre, and the city's train and main bus stations are all centrally located.

## By air

**Changi International Airport** lies at the far eastern end of the island, 16km from the city centre. As well as duty-free shops, ATM and money-changing facilities and a left-luggage area, the airport boasts a 24-hour post office and telephone service, hotel reservation counters and Internet cafés. There are also car rental agencies.

Singapore's underground train system (**MRT** – Mass Rapid Transit) extends as far as the airport, and is the most affordable means of getting into town: a trip to downtown City Hall station costs $1.40 and takes half an hour. From City Hall interchange you can move on to any part of the island. **Bus** departure points in the terminal basements are well signposted. You'll need the right money, as bus drivers don't give change; take the #36 (daily 6am–midnight, every 10min; $1.60). The bus heads west to Stamford Road, before skirting the south side of Orchard Road. **Taxis** from the airport levy a $3 surcharge on top of the metered fare, which rises to $5 on weekends. A trip into downtown Singapore costs around $15 and takes twenty to thirty minutes. Another option is to take a **MaxiCab** shuttle. These six-seater taxis, equipped to take wheelchairs, depart every fifteen minutes (or when full), and will take you to any hotel in the city for a flat fare of $7 (children $5). Both metered cabs and MaxiCabs are well signposted from the Arrivals concourse.

## By road

**Buses** stop at one of three terminals in Singapore. Local buses from Johor Bahru in Malaysia arrive at **Ban San Terminal** at the junction of Queen and Arab streets, from which it's a two-minute walk along Queen Street, followed by a left along Rochor Road, to Bugis MRT station. Buses from elsewhere in Malaysia and from Thailand terminate at either the Lavender Street Terminal or the Golden Mile Complex. **Lavender Street Terminal**, at the corner of Lavender Street and Kallang Bahru, is around five minutes' walk from Lavender MRT; bus #145 passes the Lavender Street Terminal on its way down North Bridge and South Bridge roads. From outside the **Golden Mile Complex**, take any bus along Beach Road to Raffles City to connect with the MRT system. You'll have no trouble hailing a cab at any of the terminals.

## By train

**Trains** from Malaysia terminate at the **Singapore Railway Station** on Keppel Road, southwest of Chinatown. From Keppel Road, bus #97 travels past Tanjong Pagar, Raffles Place and City Hall MRT stations and on to Selegie and Serangoon roads; alternatively, take a cab from the station forecourt.

# City transport and tours

All parts of the island are easily accessible by bus or MRT (or a combination of both) and fares are reasonable. The *Transitlink Guide* ($1.50), available from bus interchanges, MRT stations and bookshops, outlines all bus and MRT routes on the island. Taxis, too, are affordable and easily available.

If you're in town for more than a few days, you might pick up an **ez-link card** (Ⓦ www.ezlink.com.sg), a stored-value card (there is a minimum purchase of $10, with a $5 deposit) that shaves a few cents off the cost of each journey. These are valid on all public transport and available from MRT stations and bus interchanges. The $10 **Tourist Day Ticket**, again available for from most MRT stations, allows you to take up to twelve bus or MRT journeys a day (of any length).

## MRT

Singapore's clean, efficient and affordable **MRT** system has three colour-coded main lines: the north–south line, the east–west line and the new north-east line. Trains run every four to five minutes on average, daily from 6am until midnight. For information, call the **MRT Information Centre** toll-free line Ⓣ1800-3368900. **Tickets** cost between 60¢ and $1.80 for a one-way journey.

## Buses

Singapore's **buses** are slightly cheaper than the MRT, and far more comprehensive. There are two domestic bus companies: the Singapore Bus Service (SBS; Ⓣ1800-2872727, Ⓦwww.sbstransit.com.sg) and SMRT Buses (Ⓣ1800-7674333, Ⓦwww.smrtbuses.com.sg). Most **fares** are distance-related and range from 70¢ to $1.30 (80¢–$1.60 for a/c buses), though some charge a flat fare as displayed on the front of the bus. **Night buses** run along a few major routes across the island; call the hotlines above for more information. Change isn't given, so make sure you have coins.

## Taxis

There are over 18,000 **taxis** in Singapore, so you'll rarely have trouble hailing a cab. They are all metered, the fare starting at $2.40 for the first kilometre, after which it rises by 10¢ for every 225m. There are **surcharges** to bear in mind, most notably the 50 percent extra charged on journeys between midnight and 6am, and the $6–8 surcharge for taxis booked over the phone; there are also electronic tolls levied on expressways and within the CBD. If a taxi displays a red destination sign on its dashboard, it means the driver is changing shift and will accept customers only if they are going in his direction. Tourists confined to **wheelchairs** should note that SMRT Taxis (Ⓣ65558888) has ten wheelchair-accessible cabs.

## Cycling

Cycling is best avoided in the city centre, but East Coast Park, Bukit Timah Nature Reserve, Pulau Ubin and Sentosa all offer plenty of scope. See the relevant Places chapters for details of bike rental firms.

## Driving

There's no real need to hire a car in Singapore but if you insist on doing so, the following companies can oblige:

**Avis** 01-07 Waterfront Plaza, 392 Havelock Rd Ⓣ67371668 and Changi Airport Terminal 1 Ⓣ65450800, and Terminal 2 Ⓣ65428855.
**Hertz** 01-01 Thong Teck Building, 15 Scotts Rd Ⓣ1800-7344646 and Changi

## River cruises and boat taxis

Fleets of **cruise boats** ply Singapore's southern waters day and night. Trips with Singapore River Cruise (Ⓣ63366111, Ⓦwww.rivercruise.com.sg; 9am–11pm) use traditional bumboats, casting off from **Clarke Quay** and passing the old godowns where traders once stored their merchandise ($12, children $6); a slightly longer cruise begins at Robertson Quay and costs $15 (children $8).

In addition, several cruise companies operate out of **Clifford Pier**, near the CBD, offering everything from luxury catamaran trips around Singapore's southern isles to dinner on a Chinese sailing boat. Companies include Eastwind (Ⓣ63333432), Singapore Riverboat (Ⓣ63389205), and Watertours (Ⓣ65339811, Ⓦwww.watertours.com.sg). A straightforward cruise will cost around $20, a dinner special $35–50. If you don't relish the idea of an organized cruise, you can haggle with a bumboat man on Clifford Pier: if you're lucky, he'll take a group up and down the river for $50 an hour.

**Boat taxis**, run by Singapore River Cruise, hopscotch between the Merlion and Robertson Quay, with a journey typically costing $3.

Airport Terminal 2 Ⓣ65425300.
Sintat 8 Kim Keat Lane Ⓣ62952211 and Changi Airport Terminal 1 Ⓣ65427288.

## Tours

**Sightseeing tours** can be arranged with any of a number of specialist operators, or ask at visitors' centres or your hotel. Tour operators include Holiday Tours (Ⓣ67382622), RMG Tours (Ⓣ62201661, Ⓦwww.rmgtours.com) and SH Tours (Ⓣ67349923, Ⓦwww.asiatours.com.sg). Most run **city tours**, which typically take in Orchard Road, Chinatown and Little India, last four hours and cost around $30. **Specialist tours** are also available – on such themes as Singapore by night, World War II sights, Chinese opera, Asian cuisines and even feng shui; prices vary from $30 to $80 per person; ask at the Singapore Tourism Board for details. Members of the Registered Tourist Guides Association (Ⓣ63392114) charge $25–50 an hour (minimum 4hr) for a **personalized tour** – as do the guides of Geraldene's Tours (Ⓣ67375250). **Trishaws** – three-wheeled bicycles with a carriage on the back – now congregate on the open land opposite the *Summer View Hotel* near Bugis Junction on Bencoolen Street, from where they'll give you a 45-minute sightseeing ride for $50.

The **Singapore Trolley** (Ⓣ63396833) is a mock-antique bus that loops between the Botanic Gardens, the Colonial District, the Singapore River and Suntec City throughout the day, and offers one day's unlimited travel for $14.90, which includes a riverboat tour. Ideal for children (and fun-loving adults) is the **Singapore DuckTours**, an amphibious craft, which provides hour-long, land- and sea-bound tours (Ⓣ63333825, Ⓦwww.ducktours.com.sg; hourly 9.30am–7.30pm; $33, children $17) of the civic district and harbour; tours start at Suntec City Mall.

# Information

**Singapore Tourism Board** (STB; toll-free Ⓣ1800-7362000, Ⓦwww.visitsingapore.com) maintains several **visitors' centres**, including offices at terminals 1 and 2 at Changi Airport. The main downtown office is at Tourism Court, at the junction of Cairnhill and Orchard roads (daily 9.30am–10.30pm).

## Useful websites

The **Singapore Tourism Board**'s official site (Ⓦwww.visitsingapore.com) is a useful place to start, featuring a tour planner, attractions, current events, a virtual tour of the island and an accommodation search by price range.
Other useful websites include:
Ⓦ**afterdark.hotspots.com** Ratings and reviews of Singapore's latest nightspots.
Ⓦ**www.expatsingapore.com** A definitive guide to expat life in Singapore.
Ⓦ**www.getforme.com** An excellent portal to all things Singaporean, from local cuisine to info for backpackers.

Other locations include level 1 of Liang Court Shopping Centre, 177 River Valley Rd (daily 10.30am–9.30pm) across the river from Chinatown; #01-35 Suntec City Mall (daily 10am–6pm), close to Beach Road and the Colonial District; and 73 Dunlop St in Little India (daily 10am–10pm). It's worth dropping in to pick up their free hand-outs and **maps**.

A number of publications offer **listings** of events. Two of these, *Where Singapore* and *This Week Singapore*, are available free at hotels all over the island. The "Life!" section of the *Straits Times* has a decent listings section, but best of all are *8 Days* magazine, published weekly ($1.50), and *I-S*, a free paper published fortnightly.

## Finding an address

With so many of Singapore's shops, restaurants and offices located in high-rise buildings and shopping centres, deciphering addresses can be tricky. The numbering system generally adhered to is as follows: #02-15 means room number 15 on the second storey; #10-08 is room number 8 on the tenth storey. Ground level is referred to as #01.

# Festivals and events

With so many ethnic groups and religions present in Singapore, you'll be unlucky if your trip doesn't coincide with some sort of **festival**, whether secular or religious. Most have no fixed **dates**, changing annually according to the lunar calendar; check with the STB, which produces a monthly round-up of festivals in Singapore, for exact dates.

**Thaiponggal** (mid-Jan) A Tamil thanksgiving festival marking the end of the rainy season and the onset of spring. At the Sri Srinivasa Perumal Temple on Serangoon Road, food is prepared against a cacophony of drums, conch shells and chanting, offered to the gods, then eaten by devotees as a symbol of cleansing.

**Chinese New Year** (Jan/Feb) Singapore's Chinese community welcomes in the new lunar year. Chinese opera and lion and dragon dance troupes perform in the streets, while markets sell seasonal delicacies. On and along the Singapore River, the Hong Bao Festival takes place, an extravaganza of floats, fireworks, music, dance and stalls that lasts for two weeks. Along Orchard Road, there are colourful parades of stilt-walkers, lion dancers and floats.

**Thaipusam** (Jan/Feb) Entranced Hindu penitents walking the 3km from Little India to Tank Road, carrying *kavadis* – elaborate steel arches decorated with peacock feathers and attached to their skin by hooks and prongs – and with skewers spiked through their cheeks and tongues, to honour Lord Murugan (see p.104).

**Hari Raya Haji** (Feb/March) This is an auspicious day for Singapore's Muslims, who gather at mosques to honour those who have completed the *haj*, or pilgrimage to Mecca.

**Singapore Film Festival** (April) Ⓦ www.filmfest.org.sg. Movies, shorts, animations and documentaries are shown with due focus given to local and Southeast Asian moviemakers.

**Vesak Day** (May/June) Monks chant sacred scriptures at Buddhist temples to commemorate the Buddha's birth, enlightenment and the attainment of nirvana; in the evening, candle-lit processions are held at temples. Race Course Road's Sakaya Muni Buddha Gaya Temple is a good place to view the proceedings.

**Dumpling Festival** (May/June) Stalls along Albert Mall sell traditional pyramid-shaped Chinese dumplings in the run-up to the Dumpling Festival, celebrated on the fifth day of the fifth lunar month. The festival commemorates Qu Yuan, a Chinese scholar who drowned himself in protest against political corruption.

**Singapore Arts Festival** (June) Annual celebration of world dance, music, drama and art, lasting several weeks and using venues around the state.

**Dragon Boat Festival** (June/July) Spurred on by the pounding of a great drum in the prow, rowing boats bearing a dragon's head and tail race across Marina Bay.

**Singapore National Day** (Aug 9) Singapore's gaining of independence in 1965 is celebrated with a national holiday and a huge show at either the Padang or the National Stadium, featuring military parades and fireworks.

**Festival of the Hungry Ghosts** (Aug/Sept) Held to appease the souls of the dead released from Purgatory, and thereby forestall unlucky events. *Wayongs*, or Chinese street operas – highly stylized and dramatic affairs in which garishly made up and costumed characters enact popular Chinese legends – are performed, and joss sticks, red candles and paper money burnt outside Chinese homes. Paper effigies of worldly goods such as houses, cars and servants are burnt, too.

**WOMAD** (Aug/Sept) Ⓦ www.womadsingapore.com. Four-day celebration of international music, arts and culture on the lawns of Fort Canning Park.

**Mid-Autumn Festival/Moon Cake Festival** (Sept) Chinese people eat and exchange moon cakes to honour the fall of the Mongol Empire – plotted, so legend has it, by means of messages secreted in cakes. Moon cake stalls spring up across Singapore two weeks before the festival.

**Lantern Festival** (Sept) Strictly speaking a part of the Moon Cake Festival, this two-week celebration takes place in the Chinese Garden, where children parade with coloured lanterns, and cultural shows – lion and dragon dances in particular – are a common sight.

**Navarathiri** (Sept/Oct) Hindu temples such as Chinatown's Sri Mariamman Temple devote nine nights to classical dance and music in honour of Dhurga, Lakshmi and Saraswathi, the consorts of the Hindu gods Shiva, Vishnu and Brahma.

**Thimithi** (Sept/Oct/Nov) A dramatic Hindu ceremony: devotees proving the strength of their faith by running across a four-metre-long pit of hot coals at the Sri Mariamman Temple in Chinatown (see p.87).

**Deepavali (Diwali)** (Oct/Nov) Serangoon Road is festooned with fairy lights during the most auspicious of Hindu festivals. Oil lamps are lit outside homes to attract Lakshmi, the goddess of prosperity, and prayers are offered at all temples.

**Ramadan** (Sept/Oct/Nov) Muslims spend the ninth month of the Islamic calendar fasting in the daytime, to identify with the hungry. The fast is broken nightly with delicious Malay sweetmeats served at stalls outside mosques. The biggest collection of stalls sets up along Bussorah and Kandahar streets, outside the Arab Quarter's Sultan Mosque.

**Christmas** Singapore's central shopping centres vie annually for the best decorations in town, making Christmas a particularly colourful and atmospheric time for shopping.

# Entertainment



## Live music

In addition to bars and clubs listed in the Places section, you can catch performances at the following venues:

**Esplanade – Theatres on the Bay** 1 Esplanade Drive ⓣ68288222, ⓦwww.esplanade.com. Features Singapore Symphony Orchestra (ⓦwww.sso.org.sg) performances throughout the year, some of which feature renowned guest soloists and conductors; also hosts contemporary Western and Asian singing stars.

**HarbourFront Centre** Hosts international acts from time to time, as well as presenting free local gigs in its amphitheatre.

**Nanyang Academy of Fine Arts Chinese Orchestra** 111 Middle Rd ⓣ63376636. Chinese classical and folk music.

**Singapore Conference Hall** 7 Shenton Way ⓣ64403839, ⓦwww.sch.org.sg. Home to the Singapore Chinese Orchestra's performances (ⓦwww.sco.com.sg) of traditional Chinese music through the year. There are occasional free concerts.

**Singapore Indoor Stadium** 2 Stadium Walk ⓣ63442660 ⓦwww.sis.gov.sg. The usual venue for big-name bands in town.

## Theatre and performing arts

**Drama Centre** Canning Rise Fort, Canning Park ⓣ63360005. Proficient drama performed by local troupes.

**Esplanade – Theatres on the Bay** see above. Sucks up all the biggest musicals, dance and events to hit Singapore.

**Kallang Theatre** 1 Stadium Walk, ⓣ63454888. Hosts visiting companies such as the Bolshoi Ballet and touring musical productions like *Chicago*.

**Substation** 45 Armenian St ⓣ63377800, ⓦwww.substation.org. Self-styled "home for the arts" with a multi-purpose hall that presents drama and dance, as well as art, sculpture and photograph exhibitions in its gallery. See also p.70.

**Victoria Concert Hall and Theatre** 11 Empress Place ⓣ63396120. Features visiting performers and successful local performances that graduate here from lesser venues.

## Cinema

**Cathay Cineplex Orchard** 8 Grange Rd ⓣ62351155, ⓦwww.cathay.com.sg. Central and recently renovated cinema, with a swish new shopping centre constructed around it.

**Golden Village GV Grand** 03-29 Great World City, 1 Kim Seng Promenade ⓣ67358484, ⓦwww.gv.com.sg. Singapore's poshest cinema, with state-of-the-art digital sound and fully reclinable seats. Pricey at $25 a ticket.

**Lido 8 Cineplex** Level 5, Shaw House, 1 Scotts Rd ⓣ67380555, ⓦshawonline.sbmedia.sg. Five screens, including the luxurious Lido Classic.

**Yangtse Pearl Centre** 100 Eu Tong Sen St ⓣ62237529. In the heart of Chinatown, this place shows Western and Asian films.

### Buying tickets

**Tickets** for cultural events can be bought either at the venue itself, or through two ticketing agencies: Sistic (ⓣ63485555, ⓦwww.sistic.com.sg) and TicketCharge (ⓣ62962929, ⓦwww.ticketcharge.com.sg).

# Sport

## Golf

Singapore boasts a number of **golf courses** disproportionate to its size, and several are truly world-class. All the clubs listed allow non-members to play upon payment of a green fee, though all will be bulging with members at the weekend. Green fees start from around $80 for eighteen holes, but you'll pay far more than this at the island's poshest country clubs. Most clubs have their own driving range, but a cheaper option is the Parkland Golf Driving Range, 920 East Coast Parkway (Ⓣ64406726), where a long session won't run to more than $10.

If you just want to watch golf, the **Singapore Open Championship** is an annual event that attracts some big names.

**Changi Golf Club** 20 Netheravon Rd Ⓣ65455133.
**Jurong Country Club** 9 Science Centre Rd Ⓣ65685188.
**Keppel Club** 10 Bukit Chermin Rd Ⓣ62735522.
**Sentosa Golf Club** 27 Bukit Manis Rd, Sentosa Island Ⓣ62750022.

## Horse racing

Singapore's only racecourse is at the **Singapore Turf Club** (Ⓣ68791000, Ⓦwww.turfclub.com.sg), next to Kranji MRT station. As legal gambling outside the course is restricted, the annual racing calendar, which encompasses around twenty meets, is popular – the most prestigious include the Lion City Cup, the Singapore Gold Cup and the Singapore Derby. When there's no racing in Singapore, a giant video screen links the racecourse to various courses across the causeway in Malaysia. There's a strict dress code – strapless sandals, jeans, shorts and T-shirts are out – and foreign visitors have to take their passports with them. Friday cards begin at 6.30pm, Saturday's and Sunday's after lunch, and tickets cost from $3 to $20.

## Soccer

Singapore's national side draws crowds large enough to fill the 55,000-capacity National Stadium in Kallang. Tickets for national fixtures normally go on sale in the week before match days, at the National Stadium's FAS box office (Ⓣ63457111). Check the local press or Ⓦwww.fas.org.sg for details.

## Swimming

Most hotels have swimming pools, but if you're in budget accommodation, you will have to opt for either the beach or a public pool. The island's longest stretch of beach lies along East Coast Park, but you'll find the waters off Sentosa's sands much cleaner. Singapore's twenty or so **public pools** are listed in the *Yellow Pages*.

## Watersports

Sea-locked Singapore Island offers extensive scope for watersports. **Windsurfing** and **sailing** are particularly popular at East Coast Park, and best organized through Pasta Fresca Sea Sports Centre (see below for details). **Canoeing** is possible at Changi Point, East Coast Park and Sentosa Island, and costs around $10 an hour, or a couple of dollars more for a double-seater. For **waterskiing** and wakeboarding, head for the Kallang River, northeast of the downtown area, or for either Sembawang or Ponngol, in the north of the island. You can expect to pay upwards of $100 an hour.

**Pasta Fresca Sea Sports Centre** 1210 East Coast Parkway Ⓣ64495118, Ⓦwww.pastafrescaseasportscentre.com.sg/seasports. Offers affordable introductory courses for newcomers to windsurfing and sailing, while proficient non-members can rent windsurfing boards by the hour or half-day.
**ProAir Watersports** SAF Yacht Club, 43 Admiralty Rd West, Sembawang Camp Ⓣ67568012, Ⓦproairwatersports.com. Wakeboarding specialists, with a Jacuzzi in which to relax after a strenuous day's boarding.

# Directory



**Airlines** Air Canada ☎62561198; Air India ☎62259411; Air New Zealand ☎65358266; American Airlines ☎67370900; Berjaya Air ☎62273688; British Airways ☎65897000; Cathay Pacific ☎65331333; Garuda ☎62505666; KLM ☎67377622; Lufthansa ☎68355912; MAS ☎63366777; Qantas ☎65687000; Royal Brunei ☎62354672; Silkair ☎62238888; Singapore Airlines ☎62236666; SriLankan Airlines ☎62257233; Thai Airways ☎62249977; United Airlines ☎68733533.

**Airport** Changi Airport flight information ☎1800-5424422 (toll-free).

**Cookery schools** Coriander Leaf Cookery School 02-01 *The Gallery Hotel,* 76 Robertson Quay ☎67323354; Raffles Culinary Academy 02-17 Raffles Hotel Arcade, 328 North Bridge Rd ☎64121256.

**Credit card helplines** American Express ☎1800-2991997; Diners Club ☎62944222; MasterCard ☎65332888; Visa ☎64375800.

**Disabled travellers** The best resource for pre-trip advice is the Disabled People's Association of Singapore (☎68891220, Ⓦwww.dpa.org.sg).

**Electricity** Singapore's mains electricity is 220–240 volts. Plugs have three square prongs, as in the UK.

**Embassies and consulates** Australia ☎68384100; Canada ☎62253240; Republic of Ireland ☎62387616; New Zealand ☎62359966; UK ☎64739333; US ☎64769100.

**Emergencies** Police ☎999; Ambulance and Fire Brigade ☎995 (all toll-free); larger hotels have doctors on call at all times.

**Gay and lesbian** Discretion is still advisable in Singapore, as practising homosexuality is officially illegal. Enforcement of such laws seems lax however, and tends to come in waves. At night, the Singapore scene centres on Chinatown and Tanjong Pagar, where there are a fair number of bars. The best way to keep abreast of the current hotspots is to go online: Ⓦwww.sgboy.com details all the best bars and clubs of the moment; and Ⓦwww.fridae.com is a pan-Asian portal for lesbians as well as gays.

**Hospitals** Singapore General Outram Rd ☎62223322; Alexandra Hospital, Alexandra Rd ☎64722000; and National University Hospital, Kent Ridge ☎67795555. All are state hospitals and all have casualty departments. Raffles Hospital, 585 North Bridge Rd ☎63111555 is private but very central.

**Internet access** There are numerous Internet cafés in Singapore, and Internet is often available at hotels and hostels. Alternatively, Orchard Road's Far East Shopping Centre is a good place to head for. Typical charges are $3 per half-hour or $5 per hour.

**Money** The currency is the Singapore dollar, written simply as $ and divided into 100¢. Notes are issued in denominations of $1, $2, $5, $10, $20, $50, $100, $500, $1000 and $10,000; coins are in denominations of 1, 5, 10, 20 and 50¢, and $1. At the time of writing, the exchange rate was around $2.80 to £1 and $1.60 to US$1. All prices given in the Guide are in Singapore dollars, unless otherwise stated. All Singapore's banks change travellers' cheques; normal banking hours are Mon–Fri 9.30am–3pm & Sat 9.30am–12.30pm. Licensed money-changers, offering slightly more favourable rates, also abound – particularly in Arab Street, Serangoon Road's Mustafa Centre, and Orchard Road's shopping centres.

**Opening hours** Restaurants are generally open daily from around noon until 2.30pm and then 5pm to 10.30pm; significant exceptions to this rule are noted in the text. Shopping centres are usually open daily 10am to 9.30pm. Opening times for bars and clubs are noted in the text. Offices generally work Monday to Friday 8.30am–5pm and sometimes on Saturday mornings. In general, Chinese temples open daily from 7am to around 6pm, Hindu temples 6am–noon and 5–9pm, and mosques 8.30am–noon and 2.30–4pm; specific opening hours for all temples and museums are given in the text.

**Pharmacies** Guardian Pharmacy has over 40 outlets, including ones at Centrepoint, 176 Orchard Rd; Raffles City Shopping Centre, 252 North Bridge Rd; and Clifford Centre, 24 Raffles Place. Usual hours are 9am–6pm, but some stay open until 10pm.

**Police** In an emergency, dial ☎999; otherwise call the freephone police hotline, ☎1800-2550000.

**Post offices** The GPO (Mon–Fri

8am–6pm, Sat 8am–2pm) is at 10 Eunos Rd beside Paya Lebar MRT; poste restante/general delivery is here (take your passport). Post offices are normally open Monday to Friday 8.30am–5pm and Saturday 8.30am–1pm; branches opening later include 1 Killiney Rd (Mon–Fri until 9pm, Sat until 4pm, plus Sun 10am–4pm). There are also branches at Changi Airport. Singpost (ⓣ1605, ⓦwww.singpost.com.sg) does an efficient job of running mail services in Singapore. Aerogrammes cost 50¢ each, while airmail starts at 70¢ to Australasia.

**Public holidays** **January 1** New Year's Day; **January/February** Chinese New Year (2 days); **January/February** Hari Raya Haji; **March/April** Good Friday; **May 1** Labour Day; **May** Vesak Day; **August 9** National Day; **November** Deepavali; **October/November** Hari Raya Puasa; **December 25** Christmas Day

**Spas** Singaporeans have gone health-treatment-crazy over the last few years, and a raft of luxury spas have opened up to cater for them. All offer a combination of whirlpools, pools, aromatherapy and beauty treatments, massages, saunas and body scrubs – treatments range from around $155 to $350. Try Amrita Spa (06-01 Raffles City Convention Centre, 2 Stamford Rd ⓣ63364477), or Esthetica (04-17 Takashimaya Shopping Centre (291a Orchard Rd ⓣ67337000).

**Telephones** For directory enquiries, call ⓣ100; for IDD information, call ⓣ100 or 1607, or ⓣ104 for international enquiries. Calls from public phones cost 10¢ for three minutes. Singapore has no area codes. Card phones have taken over from payphones: cards are widely available and come in $3–50 denominations; you can use them to make international calls. International cards come in $10–50 denominations. IDD calls from hotel rooms in Singapore carry no surcharge. Skype or other Voice over Internet Protocol (VoIP) services are increasingly available from Internet cafés, much reducing the cost of calling abroad.

**Time** Singapore is 8 hours ahead of GMT, 16 hours ahead of US Pacific Standard Time, 13 hours ahead of Eastern Standard Time, and 2 hours behind Sydney.

**Tipping** Tipping is not customary in Singapore. Restaurants, however, automatically add a service charge and government tax (around 15 percent) to bills.

**Women's helpline** AWARE is a women's helpline ⓣ1800 7745935, ⓦwww.aware.org.sg.



## Fly Less – Stay Longer!

Rough Guides believes in the good that travel does, but we are deeply aware of the impact of fuel emissions on climate change. We recommend taking fewer trips and staying for longer. If you can avoid travelling by air, please use an alternative, especially for journeys of under 1000km/600miles. And always offset your travel at ⓦwww.roughguides.com/climatechange.

# Chronology

# Chronology

**200AD ▸** Chinese sailors may be referring to Singapore in their account of a place called Pu-Luo-Chung, "island at the end of a peninsula".

**200–1200 ▸** Singapore grows into a trading outpost of the Sumatran Srivijaya Empire, known locally as Temasek ("sea town").

**1200s ▸** Marco Polo reports sighting a place called Chiamassie, which could be Singapore.

**1390s ▸** Sumatran prince, Paramesvara, throws off allegiance to the Javanese Majapahit Empire, flees to Singapore, murders his host and rules the island until a Javanese offensive forces him north, up the peninsula, where he founds the Melaka sultanate.

**1500s ▸** First record of the island's current name (from the Sanskrit Singapura, meaning "Lion City") in the Malay annals, the *Sejarah Melayu*.

**1613 ▸** Portuguese accounts tell of the razing of an unnamed Malay outpost at the mouth of Sungei Johor; two centuries of anonymity ensue.

**1818–19 ▸** British East India Company seeks to establish a British colony at the south tip of Malay Peninsula. Colonial administrator Thomas Stamford Raffles steps ashore on the north bank of the Singapore River and strikes a treaty with Abdul Rahman, *temenggong* (chieftain) of Singapore, and Sultan Hussein Mohammed Shah, establishing a British trading station there.

**1822 ▸** Raffles draws demarcation lines that divide present-day Singapore. The area south of the river is earmarked for the Chinese; the commercial district is established at the river mouth; and Muslims are settled in today's Arab Quarter.

**1824 ▸** Singapore's trading expansion begins: Malays, Chinese, Indians and Europeans arrive in search of work as coolies and merchants; the population reaches ten thousand by the time of the first census.

**1824–27 ▸** Sultan Hussein and the *temenggong* are bought out, and Singapore is ceded outright to the British. The fledgling state unites with Penang and Melaka (by now under British rule) to form the Straits Settlements.

**1867 ▸** The Straits Settlements become a British crown colony. By now the population has reached eighty thousand.

**1877–87 ▸** Henry Ridley introduces the rubber plant into Southeast Asia; the island is soon the world centre of rubber exporting. *Raffles Hotel* opens for business.

**1942–45 ▸** Singapore falls to the Japanese and is renamed Syonan, "Light of the South". The brutal Japanese rule sees thousands of civilians executed in anti-Chinese purges, while Europeans are herded into Changi Prison or marched up to work on Thailand's

"Death Railway".

**1946** ▸ The Straits Settlements are dissolved; Singapore becomes a crown colony in its own right.

**1948** ▸ The Federation of Malaya brings together all states of Peninsular Malaya, but not Singapore, whose inclusion would have led to ethnic Malays being in a minority. Chinese opposition to the federation ignites the Communist Emergency, a guerrilla struggle lasting until 1960, whose aim is to turn Singapore and Malaysia into a republic.

**1959** ▸ Full internal self-government is achieved; People's Action Party (PAP) leader, Lee Kuan Yew, becomes Singapore's first prime minister.

**1963–65** ▸ Singapore combines with Malaya, Sarawak and British North Borneo (Sabah) in the Federation of Malaysia, but Sino–Malay tensions soon see Singapore asked to leave the federation. Lee Kuan Yew announces full Singaporean independence.

**1965–92** ▸ Per capita income increases fourfold; huge profits are made in financial services, hi-tech manufacturing, information technology and the petroleum industry. Meanwhile, "soft authoritarianism" grows: in 1972, Cliff Richard is refused entry into Singapore because his hair is too long. Twenty years later, chewing gum is banned across the state.

**1990–2004** ▸ Goh Chok Tong becomes prime minister upon Lee's retirement in 1990. Still, Lee looms over the political scene, as senior minister. His eldest son, Brigadier-General Lee Hsien Loong, becomes prime minister in 2004. On the same day, the elder Lee is named "minister mentor".

**2003** ▸ Severe Acute Respiratory Syndrome (SARS) claims 31 lives.

**2006** ▸ The People's Action Party is returned with 82 of the 84 seats in May's elections.

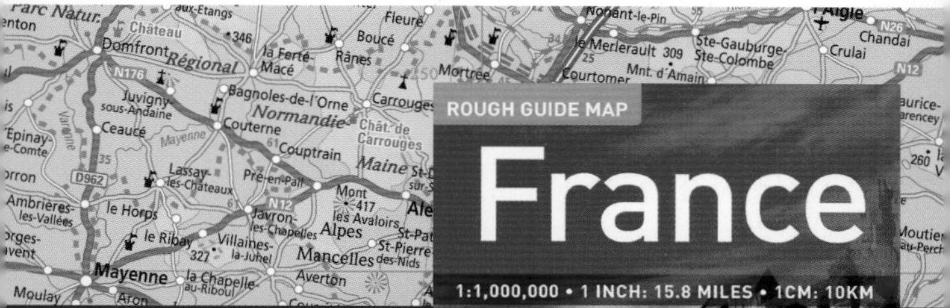

# small print & Index

## A Rough Guide to Rough Guides

In 1981, Mark Ellingham, a recent graduate in English from Bristol University, was travelling in Greece on a tiny budget and couldn't find the right guidebook. With a group of friends he wrote his own guide, combining a contemporary, journalistic style with a practical approach to travellers' needs. That first Rough Guide was a student scheme that became a publishing phenomenon. Today, Rough Guides include recommendations from shoestring to luxury and cover hundreds of destinations around the globe, including almost every country in the Americas and Europe, more than half of Africa and most of Asia and Australasia. Millions of readers relish Rough Guides' wit and inquisitiveness as much as their enthusiastic, critical approach and value-for-money ethos. The guides' ever-growing team of authors and photographers is spread all over the world.

In the early 1990s, Rough Guides branched out of travel, with the publication of Rough Guides to World Music, Classical Music and the Internet. All three have become benchmark titles in their fields, spearheading the publication of a range of more than 350 titles under the Rough Guide name, including phrasebooks, waterproof maps, music guides from Opera to Heavy Metal, reference works as diverse as Conspiracy Theories and Shakespeare, and popular culture books from iPods to Poker. Rough Guides also produce a series of more than 120 World Music CDs in partnership with World Music Network.

Visit www.roughguides.com to see our latest publications.

Rough Guide travel images are available for commercial licensing at www.roughguidespictures.com

## Publishing information

This first edition published March 2007 by Rough Guides Ltd, 80 Strand, London WC2R 0RL; 345 Hudson St, 4th Floor, New York, NY 10014, USA.

Distributed by the Penguin Group
Penguin Books Ltd, 80 Strand, London WC2R 0RL
Penguin Group (USA), 375 Hudson St, NY 10014, USA
14 Local Shopping Centre, Panchsheel Park, New Delhi 110017, India
Penguin Group (Australia ), 250 Camberwell Rd, Camberwell, Victoria 3124, Australia
Penguin Group (Canada), 10 Alcorn Ave, Toronto, ON M4V 1E4, Canada
Penguin Group (NZ), 67 Apollo Drive, Mairangi Bay, Auckland 1310, New Zealand
Typeset in Bembo and Helvetica to an original design by Henry Iles.
Cover concept by Peter Dyer.

Printed and bound in China

180pp includes index

A catalogue record for this book is available from the British Library

ISBN 1-84353-788-5

ISBN 13 9-78184-353-788-5



1 3 5 7 9 8 6 4 2

## Help us update

We've gone to a lot of effort to ensure that the first edition of Singapore DIRECTIONS is accurate and up-to-date. However, things change – places get "discovered", opening hours are notoriously fickle, restaurants and rooms raise prices or lower standards. If you feel we've got it wrong or left something out, we'd like to know, and if you can remember the address, the price, the phone number, so much the better.

We'll credit all contributions, and send a copy of the next edition (or any other DIRECTIONS guide or Rough Guide if you prefer) for the best letters. Everyone who writes to us and isn't already a subscriber will receive a copy of our full-colour thrice-yearly newsletter. Please mark letters: "Singapore DIRECTIONS Update" and send to: Rough Guides, 80 Strand, London WC2R 0RL, or Rough Guides, 4th Floor, 345 Hudson St, New York, NY 10014. Or send an email to mail@roughguides.com

Have your questions answered and tell others about your trip at www.roughguides.atinfopop.com

## Rough Guide credits

Text editor: Edward Aves
Layout: Diana Jarvis
Photography: Simon Bracken
Cartography: Jai Prakash Mishra
Picture editor: Harriet Mills
Proofreader: David Paul
Production: Aimee Hampson, Katherine Owers
Cover design: Chloë Roberts


## The author

After graduating from the University of Bristol, Mark Lewis spent a year teaching English in Singapore, during which time he regularly contributed book reviews to the *Singapore Straits Times*. Author of the *Rough Guide to Singapore* and co-author of the *Rough Guide to Vietnam* and the *Rough Guide to Malaysia, Singapore & Brunei*, Mark is now Editor of *Caterer & Hotelkeeper*.


## Photo credits

All photos © Rough Guides except the following:

Front image: Fish, Chinatown © Alamy
Back image: Movie poster © Alamy
p.1 Serangoon Road sign © Steve Allen Travel Photography/Alamy
p.6 The CBD and Boat Quay at night © Singapore Tourism Board
p.11 National Museum © National Museum of Singapore
p.14 Bush baby, Night Safari © Travis Rowan/Alamy
p.15 Singapore Turf Club © Roslan Rahman/Getty Images
p.16 City Hall © Robert Harding Picture Library/Alamy
p.17 Singapore Cricket Club © DK Images
p.24 Clubbing at Zouk © Yadid Levy/Alamy
p.25 Ministry of Sound © Ministry of Sound Singapore
p.29 Singapore DuckTours © Singapore Tourism Board
p.32 Sungei Buloh Wetland Reserve © DK Images
p.32 HSBC TreeTop Walk © National Parks Board, Singapore
p.33 MacRitchie Reservoir © DK Images
p.35 Chinese opera © Danita Delimont/Alamy
p.37 National Museum © National Museum of Singapore
p.38 Singapore Symphony Orchestra, Victoria Concert Hall © DK Images
p.38 WOMAD at Fort Canning Park © DK Images
p.39 Chinese opera © Stock Connection/Alamy
p.39 Lido 8 Cineplex © DK Images
p.40 Sentosa Golf Club © Jonathan Drake/Getty Images
p.41 Cycling, Bukit Timah Nature Reserve © DK Images
p.42 New Majestic Hotel © newmajestichotel.com
p.44 Hindu devotee during Thimithi © How Hwee Young/epa/Corbis
p.44 Dragon Boat Festival © Anthony Brown/Alamy
p.45 Chinese New Year celebrations © GP Bowater/Alamy
p.45 Mid-Autumn Festival dragon lantern © Roslan Rahman/AFP/Getty Images
p.45 Christmas in Singapore © Reuters
p.45 Hindu devotee carrying a *kavadi* during Thaipusam © Singapore Tourism Board
p.47 View from Mount Faber © DK Images
p.64 Bar and Billiards Room, Raffles Hotel © DK Images
p.70 Stained-glass dome, National Museum © National Museum of Singapore
p.72 Crazy Elephant © DK Images
p.73 Ministry of Sound © Ministry of Sound Singapore
p.79 Newton Circus Hawker Centre © Onasia.com
p.80 No.5 Emerald Hill © DK Images
p.91 Zhen Lacquer Gallery © DK Images
p.99 Post Bar, The Fullerton © The Fullerton Hotel Singapore
p.135 Lim's Art & Living © DK Images
p.136 Dining in Holland Village © Singapore Tourism Board

# Index

Maps are marked in colour

INDEX

## j



## k



## l



## m



## n



## o



## p



## r



## s

## u

## w